Keeping Your Home Safe

BY BARTON J. PALMER

READ THIS BOOK TODAY IF YOU WANT...

- **A HOME THAT'S SAFE FOR YOUR FAMILY.** ELIMINATE WORRIES ABOUT THE AIR THEY ARE BREATHING OR THE IMPURITIES THEY MIGHT BE DRINKING.
- **A HOME THAT'S MORE SECURE FOR YOUR FAMILY.** STOP WORRYING ABOUT THE SECURITY OF YOUR FAMILY IN CASES OF POWER FAILURE, POWER SURGE OR EVEN TRESPASSERS.
- **A HOME THAT'S COMFORTABLE FOR YOUR FAMILY.** IF SOME FAMILY MEMBERS ARE TOO HOT AND OTHERS TOO COLD, OR IF YOU HAVE ALLERGY SUFFERERS IN YOUR HOME, YOU CAN MAKE SURE YOUR HOME FEELS COMFORTABLE AND WELCOMING TO ALL.
- **A HOME THAT'S EVEN MORE BEAUTIFUL.** ENJOY A GORGEOUS HOME THAT FEELS LIKE A TREASURED OASIS. WHETHER IT'S A SIMPLE THING LIKE MATCHING RECEPTACLES, AN UPGRADED LIGHT OR NEW FAN, OR SOMETHING BIGGER LIKE A WHOLE NEW BATHROOM, YOU'LL FIND OUT MORE HERE ABOUT HOW TO BEAUTIFY YOUR SURROUNDINGS.
- **A HOME THAT'S ECO-FRIENDLY.** LEARN THE INS AND OUTS OF ACHIEVING AN ECO-FRIENDLY HOME AND REDUCING YOUR ENVIRONMENTAL FOOTPRINT.
- **A HOME THAT'S MORE CONVENIENT.** DISCOVER THE AMAZING POWER OF HOME AUTOMATION AND LEARN HOW TO CONTROL YOUR HOME FROM YOUR PHONE TO MAKE LIFE A LITTLE BIT EASIER.

DEDICATION

For everyone at Lion Home Service. We work. We serve.
We make a difference. I'm proud of the Lion Team.

CONTENTS

ACKNOWLEDGMENTS

I'd like to start by thanking my team members, who step up and represent Lion Home Service as experts delivering their very best to Northern Colorado families.

I'd also like to thank my own family, who support and encourage me to give my very best as I strive to inspire my team to serve our customers daily.

And, of course, I thank YOU, my valued customers. You are my inspiration and the reason my team and I show up and give our very best every single day. Your family's safety, health and comfort is our top priority and our main focus. It's a privilege to serve you.

Thank you from the bottom of my heart,

Barton J. Palmer

FOREWORD

Dear readers,

As the founder of Realities For Children Charities and a former child protection case manager for the Larimer County Department of Human Services, I've dedicated my life to providing for the needs of children that have been abused and neglected. You may be wondering what this has to do with Lion Home Service's endeavor to publish a home maintenance book, and why I'm writing this foreword. Allow me to explain the connection.

Realities For Children provides for more than 6,000 abused and at-risk children each year through emergency services, youth activities, distribution of critical items, and special programs aimed to help those recovering from abuse and domestic violence. In the nearly three decades I've worked in child protection roles, I've learned that we simply cannot do what we do alone. Making a real impact on child abuse issues requires the input and backing of our local community. Realities For Children is able to have this powerful impact because of the more than 35 collaborative partnerships we've created with the Larimer County agencies who work together to benefit at risk youth. Our network of 250 business members assists us in providing needed services, connecting our agency partners and underwriting all of our administrative costs. Thanks to all these business members 100 percent of every dollar donated to Realties For Children goes to directly benefit children in need.

For the past decade, Lion Home Service has stepped up in a big way to support our mission, both financially and through hands-on volunteer work. By committing a percentage of all sales to Realities For Children, the generous contributions Lion Home Service has been able to provide have gone a long way toward improving the lives of children in need. As a Gold Business Member since 2006, Lion has also sponsored fundraising events and to support our Bikes For Tykes program every year. They are a Cornerstone Donor in the construction of our Homebase Campus for the children we serve and the Lion Home Service team is a year round partner providing quality, on-time service for the overall maintenance of our facilities.

I am writing this foreword, because I can share from personal and professional experience when I say that Lion Home Service stands ready to provide you with the best possible care for your home, and you can be assured that you're working with a team that invests in and truly cares for the most vulnerable members of our community.

Craig A. Secher
Executive Director, Realities For Children

For a complete list of all the Realties For Children Business Members invested in our communities children please visit RealitiesForChildren.com

$2.00 from the proceeds of every book sold will be donated to Realities For Children

DISCLAIMER

If you have a medical question, you go to the doctor. If your car breaks down, you take it to a mechanic. You probably wouldn't turn to a book for answers to your specific situation.

Likewise, this book is not intended to replace analysis by and recommendations from home service experts like those at Lion Home Service.

This book is intended to serve as an introduction to the systems in your home, an inspiration to help you achieve a safer and more comfortable home, a troubleshooting guide and a tool that can help you make better decisions.

Whether you're seeking to improve your body, your car or your home, you should <u>always</u> consult an expert.

INTRODUCTION

Your home is your castle. After a long day at work, there's nothing like returning home to your family to relax around the dinner table and recharge with your loved ones.

The highlight of my day is spending time at home with my family, and I'm sure it's the same for you. The last thing you want is to have to worry about whether or not your home is safe and comfortable. When it's not, you want to take steps immediately to make it safe and comfortable again as soon as possible.

That's why I've dedicated my life to helping local families just like yours enjoy a safer and more comfortable home.

Hi, my name is Barton Palmer and I'm the founder of Lion Home Service. Here, I've built a team of trusted experts to capably assist you with any home-related services, no matter what the situation.

- Is the temperature of your home too hot, too cold or inconsistent?
- Does your faucet drip?
- Do your lights, fans and receptacles work the way they're supposed to?
- Are you doing a renovation and need help with pipes, wires or ducts?
- Are your drains backed up?
- Has the season changed and you need an HVAC system check-up?
- Is your home dusty?
- Are you concerned about water quality?

These and many other situations you may face in your home are the very things that inspired me to start my company, Lion Home Service.

I got into construction plumbing in 1998, transitioning into a Ben Franklin franchise in 2006, and adding heating and air service to the portfolio in 2013. In May 2018, my team and I launched Lion Home

Service as your complete home solution to cover heating and cooling, electrical, water treatment, insulation and other home service issues. We're proud to earn the trust of our Northern Colorado families every day by delivering on our promise of complete customer satisfaction.

Perhaps you've seen our trucks on the road or visited our web site at lionhomeservice.com. Maybe you've seen our company featured on local news stations, or read my articles in the Coloradoan and on HomeownersNewswire.com.

Everything we do is to serve you, our valued customers. Our team of local experts is available 24 hours a day, 7 days a week, 365 days a year to provide you with the services you need when you need them to make sure your family is as safe and comfortable as possible.

Why do we do this? It's simple. We live here, too. We're your neighbors and friends, and we understand exactly how important it is to keep your home safe and comfortable for your family.

We get feedback all the time from local homeowners who love the service we provide:

"The technicians were respectful, they were professional and wanted in every way to leave me as a satisfied customer; and they did!"
— *Janet W.*

"Absolutely amazing and as professional as possible. They went above and beyond in their effort to solve our water heater issues. They were friendly and knowledgeable. I wouldn't trust any other company with my home HVAC needs. 5 Stars all the way!"
— *Erin P.*

"Lion Home Service kicks butt. Total 5 star review; every time I call, they come through. Extremely happy with their services."
— *John M.*

I wrote this book because I want to equip you with the ideas, strategies, tools and decision-making criteria you need to enjoy your home and get the most out of it. My goal is to "wow" you like we've wowed the customers quoted here above and thousands of others just like them.

So whether you need an entirely new HVAC system, your home could use some simple tweaks to make it safer and more comfortable, or you'd like one of our experts to visit your home and make some recommendations, we are here and ready to serve you!

If we can help in ANY way, please don't hesitate to reach out. You'll find my company's contact information in the back of this book.

Barton J. Palmer
Owner, Lion Home Service

WHAT WE VALUE

I thought you should see this first. It's important.

At Lion Home Service, we believe in a set of Core Values that guide our decisions and actions every single day. I wanted you to see them so you'll know what we value. If you value similar things and want to work with a company that relies on Core Values like these, we might be a good fit to help make your home safer and more comfortable for your family.

Core Values — Overview

We're setting a new standard for excellence in the industry, and it starts with YOU. Every word, action and decision has the potential to benefit our clients and our team, and to contribute to our success. Embed these Core Values into your thoughts and actions and together, we'll continue to push even higher.

Core Value #1 — Safety first for our family and yours
Think twice, act once.

Our team and our clients are our greatest assets, and we value them as such! We take care of them, protect them and strive to reduce the risks they face. No matter where you are — in the office, on the road or at a client's home — examine the situation for opportunities to eliminate potential dangers.

Core Value #2 — Deliver "Wow!" through service
Exceeding every client's expectations.

There are many service companies in the market, but they're only competitors if we deliver at the same level they do. We rise above the others when we delight every customer by going above and beyond what our clients expect. This is our greatest competitive advantage.

Core Value #3 — Demonstrate the highest level of integrity
Doing the right thing, even when no one is watching.

When we work with integrity, we know that we can trust each other and that our clients can trust us. No matter is inconsequential. Everything we do is important, and it all contributes to our success.

Sometimes the right way isn't the easiest or fastest way, but we do what's right, no matter what it takes.

Core Value #4 — A great place to work
All for one and one for all.
Like rowers in a boat, our team pulls together. We each deliver to the very best of our ability, and we trust our fellow team members to do the same. When we show up to work fully engaged, inspired and ready to work as one, we become more than just co-workers. We become family.

Why do we do what we do? Our Core Purpose sums it up:

Core Purpose — To help all people live in greater safety and comfort
The work we do at Lion Home Service is essential because we're not just in the service business; we're in the business of improving people's lives. It's an exciting privilege to be part of a team that can contribute to the world in such a meaningful way, and you're an essential part of our team's contribution.

Here's what our trucks look like...

When we show up for an appointment at your home, our team members will arrive in a vehicle like this, and they'll always be wearing clean, crisp uniforms and name tags so you'll know they're <u>our</u> experts.

Look for our trucks in your neighborhood — we're serving your neighbors to keep their homes safe and comfortable for their families as well as yours!

PART 1.

READ THIS SECTION FIRST… (YOU MIGHT BE VERY SURPRISED, AND IT COULD SAVE YOU A LOT OF MONEY!)

You invest a lot in your home, and the return on that investment is worth more than money. It's safety and comfort. And when it comes to your family, you're probably willing to spend whatever's necessary to keep them safe and comfortable. Wouldn't it be nice if you could save some money along the way? Keep reading to find out how…

HERE ARE 8 REASONS WHY YOU SHOULD READ THIS BOOK RIGHT NOW:

This book was written for YOU. It's meant to help and empower you, and it was given to you by someone who cares about you and your family. Here are 8 reasons why you should read this book right now...

1. **Ensure the safety of your loved ones.** People define family in many different ways; we like to think that the people we're closest to represent ours. However you define yours and whoever it includes, you'll want to do everything you can to keep your loved ones safe. This book will lay out the best ideas, information, resources and strategies to help you achieve that goal.

2. **Enjoy a comfortable home.** Once you're assured that your family is safe, you'll also want to make sure they're comfortable. Home is an oasis from the busy world, and this book will help you create one that is welcoming and comfortable.

3. **Protect your home.** For most people, a home is one of the biggest investments they'll ever make. Of course, you'll want to protect it. Making good decisions can extend the life of your home for years to come, helping ensure your home remains intact, as well as your family's safety and comfort.

4. **Increase your home's value.** Wouldn't it be nice if you could increase the value of the investment you've made in your home so it'll be worth even more if you ever decide to sell? Many factors outside our control can influence the selling price of a house, but we know that taking good care of your home's systems and installing new system that buyers find attractive (such as a modern high-efficiency furnace or a water filtration system) can potentially increase the value of your home as compared to others on the market.

5. **Make faster, better and more confident decisions**. Today's homeowners are busy people! Between work, social life, the kids' soccer practice and your own volunteer activities, you probably don't have a lot of time in the day to waste. Decisions about your home — plumbing repairs or investing in a new air conditioning unit, for example — can be daunting and difficult to squeeze into an already crammed schedule, especially since most people don't have a lot of familiarity with these and other systems. This book will give you an overview of the systems in your house and help you figure out how best to take action. It can also help you make better, more confident decisions about what steps to take.

6. **More time**. You plug in a desk lamp and turn it on. Nothing happens. What should you do? Many people aren't sure. They might try a few different things, or call a family member or friend for help. This book can help you instantly find answers to common home service issues and troubleshoot to figure out what's wrong.

7. **Save money**. If something happens in your home, you may not be sure how to fix it. You might attempt to fix the problem yourself, or you may hire someone else who is not qualified to fix it. Ultimately, either of these choices costs you more money than having an expert fix it right the first time. Reading the information in this book will help you know exactly what to do, in turn helping you save money by making the right decision with the right expert.

8. **Less stress**. You already have enough to deal with in your day; you don't need any more worry to occupy your mind! This book will help you figure out the best decisions quickly and confidently so you can skip the stressful decision-making and get back to living your life.

We've written this book to serve you and your loved ones. Taking the time to read it can help you create a safe, comfortable and beautiful home!

HOW TO USE THIS BOOK TO MAKE YOUR HOME SAFER AND MORE COMFORTABLE

This book was written for people who own and care for homes:

- Homeowners
- Landlords
- Property managers
- Seniors
- Investors
- Insurance Agents
- Caregivers
- Those who have inherited a home
- Those who own a second home (such as a rental property, cottage or shore house)
- Renters who want to make sure their apartment, house or condo is as safe as possible, and who want to be better informed
- Real estate professionals who want to understand the inner workings of the houses they are helping others buy or sell

It doesn't matter whether you live in a house or take care of one for someone else. If you want to know how to better care for a home, keep its occupants safe and increase its value, we've written this book specifically for you. Throughout these chapters, we may use the word "homeowner" to represent YOU — the person who owns, uses and cares for the home and its occupants.

This book is non-technical, which means you don't need to have any experience with the systems described — HVAC, plumbing, electrical, etc. This book will give you all the relevant information you need to know.

This book is not intended to replace expert advice from qualified, licensed and experienced professionals. Rather, this book is meant to help you understand what you as a homeowner should know to confidently interact with a professional.

Ultimately, this book is meant to help you feel good about your ability to care for your home and ensure that it's as safe, secure, comfortable and valuable as it can be.

This book is formatted to be used in three specific ways:

1. We recommend you read this book cover-to-cover at least once to fully understand your home.
2. You can skim this book each year to build a game plan for continually improving your home.
3. You can dive into the specific sections you want to know more about. For example, if your air conditioner starts making a funny noise, simply turn to the air conditioner section of this book to learn more.

Reading this book as a whole gives you the big picture at once; skimming through on a yearly basis helps create a game plan to make your home even more safe and beautiful; and diving in here and there when necessary empowers you with a tactical approach to caring for your home.

There's one more way that this book will help you. It introduces you to me — the author and your ally when it comes to the care and safety of your home and family. Please feel free to reach out (my name and contact information is listed in the back of the book) and I'll make sure my team and I serve you at the highest level.

THIS WILL SURPRISE YOU...

Some people might look at this book and think it's simply about how to maintain and repair a house, but that's not it. You might be surprised to discover what it's REALLY about — your family.

According to a survey by the Department of Housing and Urban Development (HUD), there are currently between 125 million and 135 million houses or "housing units" in the United States. This number includes single detached houses, apartment units and mobile homes. (https://www.statista.com/statistics/183635/number-of-households-in-the-us/). That's a lot of *houses*, but there's a big difference between houses and homes.

Many of those millions of houses stand empty. Some are short-term rentals. Some are in the process of being built while others are being torn down.

If you've lived in more than one house in your lifetime, you may have called each one your home for as long as you lived there. Once you'd moved away, the structure continued to be a house, even though it was no longer your home.

So what it is that makes a house a home?

Most of us think of a house as a structure. There are walls, a roof, doors and windows.

But when you think of home, what comes to mind? For most people, a home is more than just a structure. It's a retreat from the craziness of the world that you look forward to returning to at the end of each day. A home is the smell of turkey roasting at Thanksgiving and voices around the dinner table. A home is where you can take your shoes off, slip into comfortable clothes and put your feet up. A home is where you share laughter and warmth and love. A home is where you make memories with your family.

No home is perfect, and you may not be able to relate to all of the elements we listed here. But for most people, home is a place that's all your own, away from work and community, where you can feel comfortable and safe with your family.

Family. There's nothing more important in life. That's what a home is all about — being with your loved ones, from parents and children, grandparents and grandchildren to adopted families, extended families, close friends and even furry, four-legged members!

Family makes life worth living, and we know you'd do anything for yours to ensure their safety, health and comfort.

Families may look different from house to house, but one thing remains constant — our commitment to YOUR family, whatever it looks like and whoever it includes.

I love family. I have my own family at home, and I think of my employees as family, too. Just like you, my team and I do everything we can to ensure that our families are safe, comfortable and happy. As home service providers, we've dedicated our lives to serving families in the local area to help you enjoy a safe, comfortable, beautiful and happy home.

This book isn't really about home maintenance and repair at all; it's about helping you help your family. Every page has been written with your family in mind. Every day, our team of experts shows up at our headquarters and goes out into the community to see how we can help and serve your family and others.

The building you live in isn't just a house. It's your home. And we want to keep it safe and comfortable for you and your family for years to come.

HOW TO BENEFIT FROM THE BIGGEST FINANCIAL INVESTMENT OF YOUR LIFE

Your home. For most people, it's the biggest financial investment of their lives. That's why most Americans save up for a down payment, acquire a mortgage loan and then live in that investment for at least a few years. It's why we want to have a positive financial outcome if and when we choose to sell. It's why we spend money on our homes to protect our investment and increase their value.

We protect our homes by maintaining the systems that keep them safe and comfortable. For example, we maintain the electrical system to ensure there's power whenever we turn on a light switch or plug something into the wall. We also want to ensure that our homes are safe and protected from the threat of fire due to improper wiring.

We may be able to increase the value of our homes by investing in maintenance and upgrades that are attractive to prospective buyers if and when we choose to sell. Consider your HVAC system. Home buyers are looking for homes that are easy and efficient to maintain. If you install a high-efficiency furnace and air conditioning system, you may attract buyers who are looking for a hands-free home.

These are just a few of the obvious financial reasons to invest in the care and maintenance of your home's systems. There are plenty of others as well.

We protect our wallets by maintaining our homes. A dripping faucet or an inefficient furnace costs money. Every drip that keeps you awake at night is a few cents down the drain. Day after day, those cents turn into dollars that add up on your water bill. If your furnace is inefficient, it will cost more to heat every square foot of your home, which you'll see on your heating bills. Should your water heater burst or some other home system disaster occur, you're faced with an even heftier bill to repair, replace and clean up.

Maintaining your home also protects your security in another surprising way — your health. From the water your family drinks to the air your family breathes, your home's plumbing, electrical and HVAC systems work together to keep your family healthy. If they're ignored and not maintained, your family could get sick from impurities in the air or water, and we all know the cost of healthcare expenses can quickly become astronomical. A small investment now and then to maintain and upgrade your home can help keep your family healthy.

Beyond the financial aspects, your home is an investment in your family's safety and protection from natural disasters and weather-related situations, fires, floods and intruders. When people know they're safe, they are more confident, comfortable, happy and better able to thrive in the world. A home that protects you and your family delivers a sense of confidence, comfort and security.

Your home is an investment in your own mental health and sanity, providing you with a welcoming retreat from the busy world — a priceless reward of living in your own sanctuary.

Your home is an investment in your time. A home that's not maintained and cared for can be costly and time-consuming to live in. Maintaining your home proactively by using the strategies in this book will help you to live more carefree.

Your home is an investment in the future. When you provide a safe, comfortable, beautiful, happy home for your family, you are creating an environment where your children can grow up and loved ones can thrive, giving them a safe place to call their own. This allows them to go out into the world and be successful because they have the confidence in knowing they have a safe place to live. Your home serves as a model for your children as they grow and one day move on to have children of their own. A well-maintained home is a legacy that will last.

PART 2.

HOW TO ENJOY YOUR BEAUTIFUL HOME AND MAKE IT SAFER AND MORE COMFORTABLE FOR YOUR FAMILY

Your home is your castle, so why would you ever want to settle for anything less than the best? In Part 2 of this book, we'll look at how you can make your beautiful home even more amazing to live in. You won't believe how good it feels to live in your home when you know this information. Just imagine how your family will feel when they come home from work or school and enter a safe, comfortable, beautiful home that welcomes them. You'll learn how to achieve that in this section of the book…

YOUR AMERICAN DREAM

The American Dream. It's the goal that has inspired millions of citizens since the founding of our country. Since its earliest days, the American Dream has included the newfound ability to choose your own career instead of working at a job your family or social standing pushed upon you. It's included the ability to financially ascend as high as you want, and it includes the opportunity to own your own home.

We take it for granted now, but homeownership is an amazing privilege that brought some of America's earliest settlers here. They escaped the overcrowded cities of Europe, where a home was something they'd have to rent for excessive sums. Here in America, a home was available to everyone.

Today, the American Dream is as much about homeownership as it is about your ability to rise as high as you like on the financial or social ladder. The home you own is part of your own family's stake in the American Dream.

For most of us, a home is the single biggest purchase we'll ever make in our lives, and many people need a mortgage to be able to acquire a house. There's a reason why so many of us willingly take on the debt and responsibility needed to acquire a house. Because your home is not just a structure, it's a statement that extends through history and proudly proclaims that you can choose your own path in life, and you are building an amazing future for your family.

By extension, your home is really about your family. Your family sets out each day to go to work or school and socialize, but you all return to your home as a safe and secure space away from the world outside. No wonder people call their homes their castles!

Your home isn't just a purchase. It's an investment. It's a critical concept with some surprising lessons. We understand what it means to invest financially, such as in the stock market. An investment should provide a financial return for the expenditure.

Financial Returns. Chances are, you bought your home partially because you hope it will rise in value during the time you live in it, so that it will be worth more by the time you sell it. And what makes a home such a powerful financial investment is your ability to control and direct the rise in value. A coat of paint throughout could add a few hundred dollars to the price of your house when you choose to sell it; a brand new bathroom could add a few thousand dollars.

Your home is more than just a financial investment. Yes, you take care of your home because you hope to achieve a financial gain when you sell it, but your home is much more than just the potential money you'll make. Unlike the other investments in your life, your home delivers other kinds of returns.

Safety and Security. We live in a crazy world, and every time we turn on the news, it just seems to get even crazier. Our homes have become a safe haven – a port in the stormy world we live in. When disaster strikes, when a difficulty rears its ugly head, what's the first thing we do? We head home to be with our families and make sure everyone is safe. Homeownership heightens this natural instinct.

No matter what struggles we face at work, at school or on the commute, we have feel better knowing that when we pull into our driveways, we're home. We're in a safe place where we can be ourselves, free from the onslaught of confusion and danger that runs rampant outside of our home. Your home is an investment in your family's safety and security.

Health. A healthy family is a top priority for everyone. We know that the choices we make, the foods we eat and the exercises we do all contribute to a long, healthy life. Likewise, our homes are an investment in the health of our families. Maintaining our homes actually contributes to healthier families. From water quality to air quality and waterproofing to wintertime heating, we can improve the health of our families by making careful choices about our homes.

Your home is an investment in the health and long life of your family. You make your home healthier, and the return you get is improved health for your family.

Comfort. You work hard each day, and when you come home, it's critical to have a place where you can relax and be comfortable. Our homes are a place where we can unwind after busy days. If couldn't come home to a few moments of peace and quiet, can you imagine how much harder life would be? This downtime is absolutely necessary for us to be healthy and to maintain our sanity!

Our homes are an investment in our comfort, our ability to just put up our feet and enjoy a few minutes of calm in the storms of life.

We buy homes because we want the return on investment of peace and quiet where we can recharge our batteries before going back out into the world.

Memories. Perhaps the most overlooked way that our homes are an investment is also perhaps the most important way. Our homes are places to build memories with our families. You'll look back and think fondly of time spent around the dining room table for Thanksgiving, or curled up in front of the fireplace on a winter evening. Each passing day is an opportunity to create memories that you'll cherish for years to come, after your family has changed and grown and your children have had children of their own.

Your home is an investment in memories you'll enjoy forever.

If you own a home, you've already realized a piece of the American Dream. And for many people, that piece is part of a financial nest egg that will protect and grow your family and its net worth. It makes sense to build on that privilege and legacy by caring for your home — your American Dream investment — to expand the value you can enjoy and the impact you can have.

This book will equip you with ideas, resources, tools and strategies to care for your home, and keep it safe and comfortable for your family.

YOUR INVISIBLE HOME

When you invite someone to your house for the first time, you often give them a visual cue to help them find the address. "It's the house with the blue door," or "It's the first house on the left after the park," or "It's the house with the big oak tree in front."

Although you can SEE your house and describe it, you're really only describing a small part of it. The walls and roof make up the structure of the house, but there are many things happening inside that are invisible even to you. These are the components of your home that contribute significantly to your family's safety and comfort.

These systems work 24/7, whether you're aware of them or not, and they all play an important role in your quality of life:

HVAC system. Your Heating, Ventilation and Air Conditioning is the system that primarily controls the temperature and air flow in your home. Want your house to be warmer or cooler? Does your house seem stuffy or dusty or breezy? Your HVAC system controls all of that.

Electrical system. This is the system that powers your house. It runs your kitchen appliances so you can enjoy cold and hot food. It powers your alarm clocks and it powers your entertainment devices so you can watch TV or browse the Internet. In most cases, your electrical system connects to the municipal grid, feeding in power from an outside source.

Plumbing system. This is the system that controls the flow of clean water coming into your house.

Drain/Sewer/Septic system. This system takes unwanted wastewater out of your house. In towns and cities, plumbing systems typically connect to a city grid, so the clean water you bring into your house and the dirty water you send away are part of a larger urban plumbing system. In less populated areas, you may rely on a septic system to remove wastewater.

Nearly every home in America has HVAC, electrical, plumbing and drain systems at work. In addition to these systems, there are others that some people employ for even greater safety and comfort. These systems sometimes connect to the systems above or stand alone and may include:

Waterproofing. This is a system many people overlook to keep exterior water outside your home. It includes your roof, gutters, landscaping, weeping tiles and any other waterproofing around your house.

Indoor air quality. This system can be connected to your HVAC system to improve the air quality in your home by removing allergens and other airborne impurities, allowing you and your family to breathe easier.

Water filtration. A water filtration and purification system attaches to your home's existing plumbing, providing you with cleaner, safer drinking water.

Home security and automation. These features provide a variety of tools to monitor the inside and outside of your home for trespassers, lock and unlock your house without the need for keys, and even automatically adjust your home's temperature from your cell phone.

Generators. Generators power your home when the electrical system is disrupted, for instance, when a storm knocks out the power to your neighborhood.

Your house is a series of systems that work together, similar in the way that your car's systems work together in a certain way to help you get where you need to go. It's similar to your body, too. Your body breathes, blood courses through your veins, your heart beats and the food you eat provides fuel to keep you alive.

Your house, your car and your body are all a series of systems that work together for a purpose. In the case of your home, the purpose is to provide a place where your family can be safe, healthy, comfortable and build memories.

Take Care Of Your House

When your car stops working, you take it to a mechanic. When you don't feel good, you visit a doctor.

You know you shouldn't wait until your car or your body are no longer working before you have an expert look at them. Preventive maintenance is a powerful investment to ensure your car and your body work correctly, and to address any cause for concern as soon as possible so that the problem doesn't become any more costly in the future.

Your home is the same in many respects. You take care of it to keep all the systems functioning at their highest level of performance, and preventive maintenance can make sure you identify any potential problems before they become costly hazards. Whether you're looking at maintenance or a breakdown, you need to call in an expert to fix the problem. And there probably isn't just one specialist you need to call. Often, there are experts for each system in your house. Regularly scheduled proactive check-ups will ensure that your house stays as safe and comfortable as it can be for your family.

WAYS TO MAKE YOUR HOME SAFER

As we've said, a house becomes a home because of your family, including children, extended family, friends and pets. This chapter will provide you with ideas about how to make your home safer for your family. (For additional money-saving tips, visit HomeownersNewswire.com or the web sites listed in the author's bio at the end of this book.)

Have your HVAC system checked regularly. Your HVAC system runs on electricity and, in many cases, also in conjunction with other substances like natural gas for your furnace and a refrigerant for your air conditioning unit, which can be extremely dangerous if they escape. A licensed expert should regularly inspect your HVAC system.

Clean or replace your HVAC filter on a regular basis and have your ductwork cleaned by a duct cleaning company. Although dust and debris might seem harmless, they can accumulate in your HVAC system (including the ductwork). If not cleaned regularly, you increase the risk of fire if dust comes into contact with a spark. This is rare, but you don't want to take any chances!

Keep your water heater temperature near the recommended setting. Water heater temperatures can be adjusted upward if you want your water hotter, or downward if want your water cooler. Instant hot water is nice, but very hot water can burn skin, especially for children who might want to wash their hands and don't realize how hot the water is. The recommended heat setting on your water heater is usually safe for most homes.

Install a water filtration and purification unit. We put a lot of trust in the water utility company to provide us with clean, safe drinking water, but did you know that recent EPA tests revealed that millions of Americans are at risk because the water utility companies are simply not able to keep up with water purification requirements? Municipal water filtration costs are rising faster than tax dollars and water bills can accommodate; meanwhile, infrastructure is crumbling. Take matters into your own hands by installing a water filtration and purification unit in your home. They're far more effective than those charcoal filter pitchers people keep in their refrigerators.

Install an air purification system in your home. Nothing is more important than the safety of your family. In any perilous situation, your first thought is to get your family away from the danger. But what if the danger is hidden and low-impact, and its true effect wasn't felt for years? That's what happens with indoor air quality in your home. Allergens and impurities are inhaled by family members day after day, and since there are no obvious or immediate effects, you don't even realize the harm that's taking place. Years from now, your family could face breathing challenges and increased healthcare costs because of the airborne impurities they're inhaling today. An air purification system can proactively safeguard your family's health.

Make sure all electrical systems are up to modern safety standards. When you switch on a light, you think nothing of it and simply expect the light to turn on. What you don't realize is that a powerful surge of electricity takes place in your walls to illuminate the light. In most cases, everything works as it should. However, if you live in an older home, a renovated home, a home built with copper wiring or a home that's been wired by an unlicensed electrician, you're running the risk of fire — or even electrocution — every time you turn on a light or plug something into an outlet.

Put covers over your receptacles. Sometimes light switch or outlet covers go missing. Maybe one cracks and you forget to replace it, or maybe you removed it to paint and aren't sure where it is anymore. Those covers aren't just for aesthetics only, but for safety as well, keeping little fingers from touching live wires and getting a very dangerous shock!

Get GFCI receptacles. You're probably familiar with the standard double electrical outlet with three holes. They're in nearly every home in America. What you might not know is that more homes are turning some or all of those receptacles into GFCI receptacles, which look similar, but also have a red and a black button on them. These GFCI receptacles are built to protect your family from shock if they happen to be using an electric item (such as an electric shaver or a hair dryer) and there's a surge or the device falls into water.

Add waterproofing to your home. During winter or heavy rains, moisture can work its way through nearly invisible cracks in your foundation. You might not notice it at first, but over time, it gets worse. Moisture not only damages your home, it can lead to mold growth, which is dangerous for your family to breath. In fact, visible mold can even lead a home to be condemned and declared unlivable. Protect your family by consulting an expert for basement waterproofing.

Test your home's radon measurement bi-annually. Radon is a radioactive gas that was discovered in 1899. It's odorless and colorless, but it can be inhaled and ingested via groundwater. Radon exposure has been linked to many forms of cancer and other illnesses. Still, many property owners don't think it's a problem they have to worry about. . The Colorado Department of Public Health and Environment finds approximately 50 percent of all Colorado homes have radon levels higher than the EPA-recommended 4 picoCuries per liter (pCi/L). It's a good idea to have your home or business tested regularly for radon. (https://www.colorado.gov/pacific/cdphe/understanding-radon)

Make sure carbon monoxide alarms are installed correctly. Knowing your carbon monoxide alarms are working properly is a serious matter that can literally save your life. Make sure there is at least one per each floor of your home located more than 10 feet from a carbon monoxide source. CO alarms should be installed near all bedrooms, as inhaling high quantities of carbon monoxide can quickly lead to unconsciousness and even death.

Know how to detect a natural gas leak and turn off the gas in your home. If you have natural gas appliances in your home, discovering and fixing leaks quickly can be a matter of life and death. Natural gas in its normal state is odorless; gas suppliers add a scent to it so it can be detected if there is a leak. Many people say it smells like rotten eggs. At any rate, it's strong, unpleasant and there is no mistaking it. If you smell natural gas, call your provider or 911 and make sure you know where the main valve is located and how to shut if off in case of an emergency.

We've given you a few ideas here, but there are many others. Get in touch with us and we'll send out one of our experts to advise you on additional ways to make your home safer for your family.

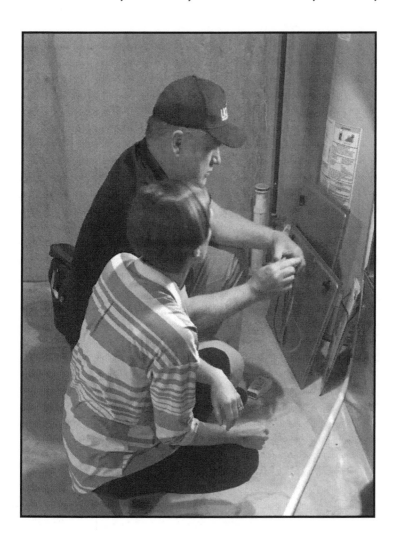

WAYS TO SAVE MONEY IN YOUR HOME

Owning a home can be expensive, and it seems like utility companies are always raising prices for water, sewer, gas and electricity. In this chapter, we'll look at some of our top money-saving ideas for your home. These are ideas we share with homeowners when we're in their homes and they ask us how they can save money. (For additional money-saving tips, visit HomeownersNewswire.com, or the web sites listed in the author's bio at the end of this book.)

Close your windows and doors when running your HVAC system. It's simple. If you want your home to be a warmer or cooler temperature than outside, you need to shut the outdoors out and allow your HVAC system to bring the indoor temperature to a comfortable level. If it's really hot outside, draw the curtains or blinds to keep the interior of your house shaded.

Check your weather stripping. Houses are not airtight. The windows, doors and vents that connect the inside to the outside are fitted to the insulation and walls. However, the seal between them isn't always perfect, so caulking or rubber weather stripping is needed to seal them up. Weather stripping deteriorates every few years, so you'll need to check and replace it periodically.

Don't run your HVAC system when you don't need it. Depending on where you live and the time of year, you may not need to run your furnace during the day when no one's home. Or, you may not need to run your air conditioner at night when everyone's sleeping. Turning off the HVAC system when you don't need it will save you money. Better yet, install a programmable thermostat to adjust the settings automatically.

Clean your HVAC air filter often and replace it regularly. Your HVAC system pushes warm or cool air through a filter, then through the ducts and into each room of your home. The dirtier your filter is, the harder your HVAC system has to work to push air through. Cleaning or replacing your filter regularly will keep the airflow moving and lower your energy bill. (Not to mention, you'll enjoy better health because the air will be free of dust and debris. A healthier lifestyle is also less costly in terms of medical bills.)

Turn down your water heater when you're away. Your water heater uses power to produce hot water on demand, but you may not always need it. If you'll be away for a weekend or longer, turn your water heater down so you won't have to pay for the energy required to keep the water hot while you're away.

Manage the heat and humidity in your attic. If you've ever had to climb into your attic in the summer, you know it gets very hot up there! And in the winter, especially in snowy climates, it gets very humid. This not only makes it harder and costlier to achieve a comfortable temperature in your home, the heat and humidity can also cause long-term damage like rot and mold. An attic fan and an attic humidistat can regulate the temperature and humidity. You may not notice the difference in your house but you'll notice the difference in your heating and cooling bills. You'll also notice a difference three to ten years down the road when your attic continues to be comfortable and dry.

Install surge protection. Chances are, you've invested money in valuable electronics, but did you know that an electrical surge can permanently damage those devices? All electricity coming into your house surges throughout the day, and sometimes those surges can be quite dramatic, especially during a lightning strike or when the power comes back on after it goes out. Unfortunately, not all home insurance covers power surges. The best solution is to install a whole-home surge protection (not ineffective surge-protecting power bars). You'll save money the very first time a surge runs through the neighborhood, destroying everyone else's electronics except yours.

Install a sump pump. Nothing's worse than waking up in the middle of a stormy night and hearing water rushing into your basement from a backed-up storm sewer or overloaded weeping tiles. A sump pump removes water before it can enter your home, helping keep your basement dry, saving you money and heartache.

Check and update your insulation. According to the U.S. Department of Energy, few attics are adequately insulated. Poor attic insulation may not seem like a big deal, but when heated or cooled air escapes from your home, your HVAC system is forced to work harder to maintain a comfortable temperature. Adding blown-in insulation is a cost-effective means of protecting virtually any attic. It can be installed by itself or over existing attic insulation as long as the older insulation is in good condition. And, it requires no maintenance, lasts as long as you own your home, and makes a significant difference on your energy bills.

Have your water heater inspected, serviced and replaced regularly. It's easy to forget about your water heater as long as hot water is flowing, but older water heaters run less efficiently, are more costly to operate, and are can be at risk of bursting. You don't want gallons of hot water spilling all over your basement floor, so have an expert service your water heater regularly.

Install an automated thermostat. One great way to save money is to only raise the temperature in your home when you need it to be warmer, and lower it when you're sleeping or away. The problem is, it's easy to forget to make these adjustments. An automated thermostat — one with pre-set adjustments or one of those cutting-edge, Wifi-enabled thermostats that "learn" your routines and can be controlled from your cell phone — allow you to adjust the temperature conveniently, saving you money.

Want to save more money in your home? We've given you a few ideas here, but there are many others out there. Get in touch with us and we'll send out one of our experts to advise you on some additional ways to save money.

WAYS TO MAKE YOUR HOME STRESS-FREE

Life can be stressful, even at the best of times, and owning a home can make life even more stressful! Imagine waking up to a funny sound, only to discover that your water heater has burst and hot water's flooding into your newly renovated basement. Or, imagine arriving home one cold winter evening only to discover that your HVAC system isn't working properly and your home is freezing cold. Or, imagine lying awake at night, knowing you have a very important day at work tomorrow only to hear the drip-drip-drip of a leaky faucet.

Here are a few ways to reduce the stress of worrying about your home. (For other ideas, visit HomeownersNewswire.com or the web sites listed in the author's bio at the end of this book.)

Have an expert check your HVAC system at least twice a year. Your HVAC is a complex system that produces hot and cold air. Around the time when you switch over from hot to cold in the spring or cold to hot in the fall, you'll want to have a licensed expert check your HVAC to ensure your system runs all season long. The last thing you want is to get home and discover that your furnace hasn't been running while you were at work, and now your house is cold and your pipes might be frozen.

Have an expert check your home's electrical system at least once a year. Your home's electrical system powers everything that makes life comfortable and convenient. Over time, this system can degrade or become less useful. Perhaps your electronic needs change and you find yourself plugging more devices things in. An expert can help solve little problems, like a receptacle that stops working, and prevent bigger problems, like an electrical fire.

Have an expert check your home's plumbing system at least once a year. Your plumbing system brings in fresh water from the supply (usually your municipal system or a well). This water is under pressure, which mean that your plumbing can spring leaks. In the winter, your pipes could be at risk for freezing. Avoid leaky pipes (and the costly mess that they entail) by having a plumber inspect your pipes and faucets every year.

Have an expert check your drain and sewer/septic system at least once a year. Your drain system removes wastewater to the municipal sewer system or to your septic system. Over time, these systems can get clogged (and septic systems can fill up). Shifting ground or nearby trees can also cause serious problems with your drain pipes. An expert should check this system at least once a year to clear your lines, empty your septic tank (if applicable) and diagnose any potential problems that need to be addressed.

Install a water filtration system in your home. Your water supply may be compromised without you even realizing it. Are you worried about the water your family is drinking? You know everyone needs to stay hydrated, but what about the quality of that hydration? Water filtration systems will eliminate the stress so you know you're providing the cleanest, healthiest drinking water for your family.

Install a whole-home surge protector. Power surges happen often. Most are relatively harmless, but more powerful surges can take place during a storm or after a power outage. When that happens, your valuable electronics could be permanently damaged, and may not be covered by your homeowner's insurance. A whole-home surge protector provides the best protection against surges. Surge-protector power bars won't always do the job; a whole-home surge protector is built to withstand electronics-damaging surges.

Install a whole-home generator. A power outage is one of the most stressful things to experience. You don't realize how much you rely on power until it goes out! Then you wonder how long the outage will last will go on, whether the food in your fridge will spoil, and if your family will be warm enough or your pipes will freeze. End the stress with a whole-home generator that connects right to your home's power system. You'll never worry about outages again, and your home will be the only one on the block that's all lit up while the rest of your neighbors' houses are dark.

Install a whole-house fan. In moderate climates, a whole-house fan can reduce your need for air conditioning except for on the hottest days. To cool your house, a whole-house fan uses powerful suction to pull air from all parts of your home, creating cooling circulation. Whenever the outside temperature drops below the indoor temperature, open some windows and turn on the fan to pull cool, dry air through the house and exhaust hot air through the roof vents. Whole-house fans are generally more effective in multi-story homes than single levels.

Install home-automation technology. Until recently, the idea of home automation was relatively unfamiliar to most people. As products and technologies have become more accessible, homeowners across the country are upgrading their homes accordingly. Simply, home automation puts the control of basic home systems and appliances into the hands of the homeowner, providing access from a remote point like a Smart phone. Just like on "The Jetsons" or "Star Trek," it's now possible to control your home's temperature, lighting and even security system with the touch of a screen, the swipe of a finger or the sound of your voice. Home automation offers security, energy efficiency, savings, convenience, comfort and peace of mind.

Want to make your home even more stress-free? Get in touch with us and we'll send out one of our experts to recommend some additional ideas.

PART 3.

A QUICK DIVE INTO YOUR HOME'S SYSTEMS AND HOW TO ENSURE THAT YOUR HOME IS AS SAFE AND COMFORTABLE AS POSSIBLE

You're enjoying a quiet evening at home when suddenly you hear a strange noise. You think it might be coming from your basement. Is it the HVAC system? The water heater? The circuit panel?

Knowledge is power. When you read this section of the book, you'll be equipped to understand your home and make the right decisions to keep it functioning in the best condition. You'll get some ideas about how to improve your home, too!

YOUR HOME'S SYSTEMS

This chapter gives you a quick, friendly overview about your home's systems so that you can understand how everything works together to help your family enjoy a safe, comfortable living environment.

Most homes in America have an HVAC system, a plumbing system and an electrical system. Where does it all start, and how does it work together?

- **Your HVAC system** provides heating, cooling and air flow (ventilation).
- **Your electrical system** powers your home.
- **Your plumbing system** brings water into your home.
- **Your drain/sewer/septic system** removes wastewater from your home.

These main systems work cohesively to ensure your home is as safe and comfortable as possible. In most cases, these systems utilize a natural source or one provided by your local government. For example:

- Your HVAC system may be supplied by natural gas or electricity through your local government. Many homes have a furnace that runs on electricity, but uses natural gas to provide the heat, along with an air conditioning unit powered by electricity. Some homes employ other methods of heating, such as electricity or oil.
- Your electrical system may connect to a local electrical supply provided by a utility company.
- Your plumbing system may connect to a freshwater supply from a well or a local government-supplied water source, and it may connect your sewer drain to a government-maintained sewer system or to a septic system.

There may be some exceptions, but these are very common sources. Once you receive the gas, water and power from the supplying source, it connects to your house and is routed to the appropriate systems by pipes (in the case of gas or water) or wires (in the case of electricity).

- Your HVAC system brings in natural gas and/or electricity to warm and/or cool your home.
- Your electrical system runs wires inside your walls to light switches and outlets (also called receptacles) to supply power whenever you need it.
- Your plumbing system runs water through pipes inside your walls to the faucets, so you can turn on the tap and get water.
- Your sewer line drains wastewater through pipes to a local sewer line, or to a septic tank or septic field.

All of these systems work (mostly) behind the scenes in your walls and under your cupboards, in wires above the street or in pipes below the street to keep your home comfortable. You barely notice them, unless they stop working for whatever reason.

For the most part, you don't need to know the details of how they work — it can take years of licensing and qualification to fully understand these systems. However, it's helpful to generally know what's happening so you can take action quickly if you want to make a change or if there's a problem with your home.

On the pages that follow, we've shared some ways to make your home safer and more comfortable.

STRATEGIES FOR YOUR SAFETY
AND COMFORT

In the last chapter, you read about the main systems in your home that keep it safe and comfortable for your family, from heating, cooling and electricity to plumbing and drains, these systems work around the clock to make sure your home is as safe and comfortable as possible.

When people need an expert to work on these systems, they call us. But these aren't the only features in your house that contribute to your family's safety and comfort. In fact, there are many other home safety and comfort strategies that we can help you with as well.

Our team of experts specializes in all the strategies, systems, techniques and services that ensure your home stays safe, comfortable and beautiful, while also retaining its value and helping to protect the environment.

On the next several pages, we'll describe a few of our most popular services. If it has to do with your home, we can either take care of the problem ourselves or recommend another qualified company to get the job done.

Check out these strategies to see what you might need right now, or if any inspire you to think about getting some work done in the future. You might read this list and think, "Oh! I want that in my home!" or "I didn't realize that needed to be maintained." Either way, we're here to help.

And don't worry — you don't need to know ahead of time if one of these services is right for you. Our experts can help you figure out the best approaches and offer recommendations on how to make your family safer and more comfortable.

Turn the page with your home in mind and start dreaming about improvements you can make. We'd love to help.

HVAC INSTALLATION AND REPAIRS

Heating, Ventilation and Air Conditioning (HVAC) systems should help you achieve an optimal temperature in your home by warming the interior when it's cold outside and cooling the interior when it's warm outside. HVAC systems also move the air around your home to keep it from becoming stale and to deliver fresh air to all rooms in your home.

An HVAC expert can repair your existing system and make sure it's in optimal working condition, or install a new system including high-efficiency features and/or special filters to clean the air and reduce allergens in your home.

ELECTRICAL REPAIRS AND RENOVATIONS

The wires in your home are usually unseen as they deliver power to receptacles and lights. Over time, they may stop working. Perhaps a circuit gets overloaded, the house shifts and pulls the wire from an outlet, a renovation accidentally cuts through a wire or a receptacle burns out due to dust or extreme use.

Along with electrical repairs, your home may have its own unique electrical needs that can change over time. Maybe you need more receptacles now than you needed years ago because more family members are charging phones, tablets and laptops.

A licensed electrician can help you by repairing the wiring and receptacles that are no longer working and by rewiring your home during a renovation to meet your evolving electrical needs.

PLUMBING REPAIRS AND RENOVATIONS

There's a lot of water going into your kitchen and bathrooms. From sinks, dishwashers and water dispenser supply lines to bathtubs, showers and toilets, all of these pipes are under pressure, which can lead to leaks or bursting. An expert can inspect these lines from time to time to make sure they remain intact, and repair them if they leak or burst.

Perhaps you're planning to remodel your kitchen or bathroom. Moving any of your fixtures or appliances that need water should involve a plumbing expert to relocate the pipes.

DRAIN CLEARING

Drains that aren't clearing can be a hassle. This situation can be caused by a clog in the pipes from something that was inadvertently put down the drain, a tree root or a bend in the pipes that can happen over time.

Some people try to fix the problem by putting harsh chemicals down their drains; others prefer to simply call an expert who can take care of it right away. Those harsh chemicals can be extremely dangerous to handle and inhale, and they may not always solve the problem.

An expert, though, can safely identify the problem — including the root cause, which may not be solved by harsh chemicals; clear your drains and, if necessary, recommend repairs to keep it from happening again.

WATERPROOFING

Basements are built strong, but they can still crack over time, allowing moisture to seep in. This can result in mildew, mold and even flooding. Unfortunately, some insurance companies don't cover all types of basement flooding or mold depending on the cause.

The best solution is to have an expert assess your basement and recommend a waterproofing solution that gives you the confidence in knowing the space will remain warm and dry all year long.

SURGE PROTECTORS

Power surges through your electrical wires all the time. Usually, these surges are minimal and your electronics can handle them, but sometimes, the surges can become too much for your electronics, such as during a lightning strike or right after an outage when the power comes back on. During a major surge, a lot of electricity travels through the wires and can permanently destroy your electronics. Your home insurance may or may not cover damage caused by these surges, and surge protector power bars are often inadequate for the most damaging surges.

Contact an expert and ask about whole-home surge protectors designed to protect all your electronics at once and give you the confidence that your home is protected, knowing you won't be inconvenienced during the next surge.

WHEN YOU NEED
ELECTRICAL SERVICES
IN NORTHERN COLORADO
DEPEND ON OUR SERVICE
EXPERTS

SUMP PUMP

In heavy rains, water that collects will drain into your weeping tiles and ideally flow away from your house. However, very heavy rainfall, degrading in your weeping tiles or municipal sewer system backups can lead to flooding in your basement.

A sump pump is designed to help protect against this flooding by collecting any backed-up water and pumping it far away from your house. I believe a sump pump should be recommended for every home, because you never know when the next rainfall, snowfall or sewer backup is going to happen.

An expert can install a sump pump, and you'll have the peace of mind in knowing that your home is protected.

SOLAR

Electricity is expensive and it seems like the cost is always rising. Wouldn't it be nice to minimize your electricity bill by tapping into a free, ecologically friendly energy source?

Solar power is free power from the sun, and it's accessible every single day of the year. You can harness that power and enjoy the savings through lower electricity bills. Plus, you'll love knowing that you're a little less dependent on non-renewable energy sources.

An expert can advise you on the best solar power solutions for your home and help you understand where solar energy collectors can go and advise you on how to store and use solar power. You'll feel good knowing that your home safe and comfortable, and you'll also be contributing to an environment that your children's children can enjoy.

GENERATORS

Have you ever been annoyed by a power outage and worried that your food in your fridge might spoil? A whole-home generator connects to your home's electrical system and starts running as soon as the power goes out, providing your home with power even if the rest of your neighborhood is dark. Your family will be comfortable, your fridge will keep running and your sump pump will have power.

An expert can install a generator to work with your home's electrical system. If you ever need to sell, imagine how much more valuable your home will be to prospective buyers when they see that the house will never be without power.

DUCT CLEANING

Ducts run through the floors and walls to deliver hot or cold air from your furnace and/or air conditioning system to each room of your home.

Over time, dust and airborne debris can build up inside these ducts (even if your HVAC system has a filter). That dust blows out of your vents into each room, making it more difficult to breathe, especially for allergy sufferers, and making your house dusty. Cigarette smoke or pet dander can travel around your home through your ducts, too, even if you're careful about where you smoke or where your pets stay.

The solution is to have your ducts cleaned at least once a year by an expert who has the tools and strategies to do a thorough job. Too many people have their ducts cleaned too infrequently. You'll love the difference it makes. And, duct cleaning can also lower your energy bill by reducing the amount of dust your furnace filter has to collect, lowering the work your system has to do.

HOME SECURITY

We've talked a lot in this book about keeping your home safe for your family. Dangers lurk everywhere, from water and air quality to external factors like burglars. You only need to watch the news for a few minutes to know that things are crazy out there, and getting more and more dangerous every day.

A home security system provides peace of mind in knowing that your family is protected. With video cameras, keyless entry, panic buttons and around-the-clock monitoring, there are many options and choices that can help to keep your family safe.

An expert can assess your current situation and advise you on how to provide a home security solution that will help your family sleep well at night.

HOME INSPECTION

If you're thinking about buying a new home to live in, as a second home or as an investment, home inspectors are highly trained experts at investigating the aspects of a house that you never see or notice. They can spot hazards, dangers and opportunities to make your home even safer and more comfortable for your family.

Most people get a home inspection during the purchase or sale of a house, but you may also want to proactively arrange for a home inspector to look at your house during other times too, to ensure it continues to be as safe and comfortable as possible. The inspector will make sure you know exactly what they're looking at and recommend specific steps you can take to improve your home.

APPLIANCE REPAIR

Your appliances a lot of use, and you don't really think about them very much until they stop working. Your stove, fridge, dishwasher, freezer, or washer and dryer are essential to keeping your family as comfortable as possible. It's inconvenient when they stop working, and buying replacements can be costly.

Fortunately, appliance repair experts are at your service to determine how to get your appliances back in working order as quickly as possible. They'll save you time, money and convenience, and you'll be back to fresh hot food, clean dishes, and clean clothes before you know it.

WATER FILTRATION

Most people don't give a lot of thought to the water that comes out of their taps, but they should. The EPA has found that millions of Americans are at risk of consuming potentially dangerous quantities of various contaminants. Some of these contaminants are never filtered out of the system, others are picked up along the pipes that lead to your home. The water from your faucet may taste clean, but it could have picked up hazardous chemicals from a source miles away that the city water department wasn't able to filter out. This happens more than people realize. (https://www.usatoday.com/story/news/2017/08/14/63-million-americans-exposed-unsafe-drinking-water/564278001/).

Charcoal filters in refillable jugs might remove some impurities, but they don't remove everything that could be endangering your family. And bottled water may be sourced from questionable local sources.

A water filtration and purification system installed by an expert is the best solution to ensuring that your family gets the purest, safest and best-tasting water possible. There's simply no other way to make sure your family's drinking water is safe.

HOME AUTOMATION

Imagine this. You're headed home after a long day at work. You know the house has been empty all day and it's probably sweltering inside. Or, maybe you're heading out of town for the weekend and your spouse asks whether you remembered to turn down the water heater

Home automation can eliminate these concerns, making your life much more convenient and stress-free while also saving you money.

With home automation, you can control your home systems from your cell phone, including your furnace and air conditioner, water heater, stove, lights and security cameras. Some home automation systems use a high-tech device that "learns" your family's habits and adjusts your home's comfort levels according to the way you live.

A home automation expert can help you figure out which tools, devices and strategies work best for your family.

INDOOR AIR QUALITY

If you've ever worried about the air your family is breathing, you'll want to look into some Indoor Air Quality (IAQ) strategies for your home. From allergens and toxins to dust and dander, there are a lot of impurities in the air. Not all impurities are necessarily dangerous, but many can lead to headaches, allergies, insomnia, sinus congestion and other health issues. Your family shouldn't have to live with those discomforts when the problem can be easily fixed.

Indoor Air Quality experts can help you find the right combination of IAQ strategies for your home and situation. You'll be amazed at how much better you and your family feel when you're breathing easier.

HANDYMAN SERVICES

There are always projects to do around your home. Maybe you want to finish your basement, add another bathroom, fix a door or repair a wall. You probably don't have the time, energy or desire to complete these projects yourself. Or, you may not feel you have the necessary skills to complete the job.

Our handyman services can help you cross things off that honey-do list once and for all without ever having to lift a hammer yourself. We can provide qualified experts to help you with any job, small or large.

HOME ENERGY AUDITS

Every time another energy bill arrives in the mail, it seems higher. Small design flaws, degraded insulation or cracks caused by settling can all make your home less energy-efficient.

A home energy auditor will go through your house and look at all the ways it could be made more efficient, from the way your blower motor runs and your attic design and layout, to the age and quality of your caulking and weatherstripping.

A home energy audit can save you a lot of money over the years by finding ways to seal up your home to keep the exterior climate outside and the warm or cool air inside.

SEPTIC AND SEWER SYSTEMS

When water runs down your drain or toilet, where does it go? There are exceptions to this rule, but in most municipal areas, it enters a local sewer system and in less-populated areas, the wastewater enters a septic system.

If you need a septic system built for your home, or if you need to connect your home to a municipal sewer system, an expert should take care of that job for you. This is not a process you want to try to tackle on your own.

A properly installed system will generally be free of problems, although you may need occasional drain clearing. All septic and sewer systems should be checked periodically to ensure settling hasn't moved or cracked the pipes.

WATER, FIRE AND SMOKE RESTORATION

Life doesn't always go as planned, and sometimes the unexpected happens. If your home has experienced fire, water or smoke damage, you'll want a restoration expert to analyze the situation and create a restoration solution for your home.

Different situations may require different solutions. For example, fire damage could lead to unknown dangers with exposed wood or wires, while unaddressed water damage could lead to mildew or mold. Often, simply scrubbing the impacted area with soap and water isn't enough.

Whether the damage is minor or extensive, a restoration expert can help you get your home back to a safe, comfortable and beautiful condition again.

SIDING

When your home was first built, it looked beautiful and perfect, but over time, weather and other factors can take their toll. Siding can get dirty, become cracked or broken, or pull away from the structure.

Whether you're fixing broken siding, upgrading your existing siding or adding new siding to reface your entire home, an expert can take care of the job for you. A siding expert knows exactly what to do to repair or replace the siding, and can advise you on what siding will best stand up to the demands of your lifestyle.

You'll love how new your home looks when the siding is complete.

ROOFING

The roof of your home bears the most brunt from Mother Nature — scorching sun, freezing snow and ice, pounding rain and shearing wind. After a few years of this abuse, your shingles will start to show wear and tear and their protective qualities will diminish. Some will loosen; others might tear and come off completely. Soon, you could have rain or snow entering your house through your roof.

A roofing expert can keep your home dry and damage-free by making sure your roof is in the best state of repair and fully operational. These experts won't just look at the shingles, either. They may be able to help you with roof boards, heat or humidity problems in your attic, and waterproofing and flashing around chimneys and pipes.

You'll probably only need to change your shingles every 15 to 20 years, but you may want an expert to examine your roof more frequently to ensure it stays in peak condition.

AWNINGS

Without any cover, the sun can shine directly through your windows and increase your home's indoor temperature. Even with curtains or blinds, your house can still get hot, and the sun can fade furniture, pictures and paint on the wall. On the hottest days, who wants to sit outside on the back deck in the blistering sun?

Awnings placed over windows, doors and decks can provide a solution. They create protective shade to keep your home cool and colors vibrant (no more faded furniture!), and also allow you to enjoy a cool, shaded deck with the family.

An awnings expert can discuss your needs and recommend some of the best solutions to provide shade wherever you need it.

PAINTING

Exteriors, wood trim, indoor rooms — much of your home is probably painted. But, paint doesn't last. It fades with the sun and chips or flakes with wear. Colors go in and out of style, and paint can lose protective qualities like waterproofing or sealing over time. Sometimes, you just want the clean, new look that only a fresh coat of paint provides.

Don't spend your own precious time on a process that can be time-consuming, messy, smelly and stressful. Talk to a painting expert who can bring in team members and complete a painting job in a fraction of the time it would take you to do it. We'll even clean up afterward!

FLOORING

Your floors take a lot of abuse each and every day. From the moment you move into your home and haul heavy furniture and appliances across it to foot traffic every single day, your floors receive tons of wear and tear. You spill things on them, the kids play on them and the pets run over them. Floors that stand up to a lot of daily activity will eventually need to be upgraded.

If you're renovating your home to add value, or your children have grown up and moved out, you may want to consider floors that are less about durability and more chic to match new décor.

A flooring expert can advise you on the best flooring for your needs make suggestions about how to improve the look, comfort and value of your home through flooring choices. You'll be amazed at the difference new flooring can make in your home.

GARAGE DOORS

Standard one-piece metal garage doors are common, but can become dented or chipped from heavy use and exposure to the elements. Perhaps you're thinking about upgrading your garage door to a multi-panel version or a beautiful carriage style model.

If you want to replace or upgrade your existing garage door, an expert can help you find the right one, choose the right locks, and install remote garage door openers for added convenience. You'll love pulling into your driveway at the end of the day and pressing the button to see your new garage door open.

Less efficienc[y] results in **higher** utility bills

INSULATION

Does your home get cold very quickly in the winter after the furnace shuts off? Does it get hot very quickly in the summer after the air conditioner shuts off? You might need to add or upgrade your insulation.

Insulation can be added in floors, walls, ceilings and attics to moderate the interior temperature of your home and protect it from exterior temperature extremes that can lead to problems like frozen pipes. It also helps absorb sound to make your home a quieter sanctuary.

Even if your home was built with insulation, it's possible that the insulation might have settled or degraded over the years. An expert can advise you on various insulation options that will protect your home and keep your family comfortable.

HOME THEATERS

Home theaters are a big trend right now. Families are no longer content with one small black-and-white TV in the living room like your parents or grandparents viewed. Today, families are setting aside entire custom rooms for high-tech home theater entertainment with soundproof walls, comfy reclining chairs, widescreen TVs (or even projectors) and crystal-clear surround sound.

If you're thinking about adding a home theater to your house, an expert will help you figure out how to best achieve the experience you want and work within your budget to find the best arrangement for your family.

POWER WASHING

You might not even notice it, but over time, stubborn layers of dust and grime can amass on the exterior walls of your home, and this build-up won't come off just with a garden hose. Power washing your home, your deck and even your driveway will instantly give your home a fresh, clean appearance that shines in your neighborhood.

You can do the job yourself, but power washing can be a messy hassle. Why not let our power washing experts take care of it for you with their own high-tech equipment? You may want your home power washed every year once you see what a difference it can make.

GUTTERS AND LEADERS

Your roof covers a wide area of your property. When it rains or when the snow melts, gutters and leaders work together to channel water from your roof and away from your home in a controlled fashion. With gutters in place, water cascades off the roof down the leaders and drains a safe distance from the structure. Without a gutter in place, water just runs off your roof and collects at the foundation of your home where it can potentially flood your basement.

If you don't have gutters or leaders, or if yours have been damaged, you need to get them fixed as soon as possible. Gutters and leaders should be checked and cleaned regularly, and may need to be patched, repaired or replaced if they develop holes or pull away from your home. An expert can look at your gutters and advise you on the best steps to remedy any problems.

HOME CONSTRUCTION

Are you thinking about doing a major renovation on your existing home or having a new home built? This is a big undertaking you should leave to professionals who know the right steps to take, the permits required and the best strategies to use in the climate in which you live.

You don't need to know ahead of time what your full plan is. Simply let the home construction experts know what you'd like to do and they can walk you through the steps and timeline required to achieve your goals, helping put together a plan and budget that fits your needs.

KITCHEN AND BATH REMODELING

Over time, your lifestyle changes. Kids grow up, and home design trends and tastes evolve. Maybe you want to update and upgrade the rooms you use most often, or maybe you're thinking of selling your home and want it to look clean, modern and attractive to prospective buyers.

Like a lot of our clients, you may have tolerated a kitchen or bath that wasn't what you really wanted for a long time. Now, your tastes, budget and lifestyle have changed and you're ready to upgrade to the beautiful, functional, stylish version of your dreams.

There are remodeling strategies for every budget and every lifestyle, from extremely simple plans that can be completed in a day or two all the way up to major remodeling. A kitchen and bath remodeling expert can explain your options and work with you to find the very best solution for your needs.

LION HOME SERVICE

A leaky, running toilet wastes more water than a dripping faucet.

Solving toilet problems by repairing a leak can save hundreds of gallons of water a day.

WINDOW AND DOOR REPLACEMENT

The windows and doors of your home serve an important purpose. Not only do the doors let you in and out, they also protect you when locked. Windows let sunlight in and allow you to see outside, and they also protect you from the elements and act as security devices. In addition, well-chosen windows and doors add beautiful design details to your home.

Choosing the right windows and doors isn't something you can do in a few minutes at a home renovation store. There are so many considerations, from climate to security and design. If it's time to upgrade your windows and doors, a replacement expert can help you understand your options and show you the best solutions for your lifestyle and situation.

FENCING

As the saying goes, "Good fences make good neighbors." Fencing provides you with security and privacy, keeps your family safe and secure, and turns your yard into a beautiful, private retreat. Metal, plastic or wood — there are fencing options for every lifestyle and budget. However, there might be other factors to consider as well, such as municipal bylaws, property lines and how you plan to use your yard.

A fencing expert is the best person to talk to about how to add, repair, replace or upgrade a fence around your yard. You'll love the impact a fence can make on your privacy and on the look of your home.

MASONRY

Once you realize what a masonry expert can do in and around your home, you'll probably start making a long to-do list. A masonry expert can improve the strength and structure of your home with brick repairs and replacement, and in some cases, foundation repair. In your yard, a mason can build retaining walls or install, repair and replace concrete steps. These experts can also create strong, beautiful, long-lasting driveways and walkways, as well as indoor or outdoor fireplaces and patios.

Wherever brick or concrete can be used, a masonry expert can provide solutions.

LANDSCAPING

As you think about the safety, comfort and beauty of your home, don't forget that the same concepts extend to the land around your structure as well. Landscaping provides functional solutions like grading to control flooding and aesthetic solutions like gardens, tree-planting and more.

Landscapers can provide one-time or year-round service to create a beautiful yard and keep it looking pristine in every season. Do you know which flowers and trees grow best in your geographic region and in the sunlight and shaded areas around your home? Using various techniques, a landscaper can create a showstopping yard that will have your envious neighbors slowing down to take a longer look, as well as a beautiful, relaxing, private retreat in your backyard where you'll want to spend time with your family.

TREE SERVICE

Trees add tremendous value to your home. Sometimes that value is financial if you live in an area where trees are a desirable commodity to have on your property. Even the shade and beauty that a tree can provide, not to mention the squeals of laughter as children climb and play, are assets. Sure, you have to keep an eye on them, clean out your gutters and rake leaves in the fall, but make no mistake about it. Trees are wonderful features to have on your property.

Like all living things, trees need to be cared for. They can often function on their own, but if you want your trees to become more beautiful and valuable to your home, employing a tree service is the way to go.

A tree service expert can provide you with strategies and resources to create stronger and more beautiful trees by recommending fertilizer blends, pruning or even safely chopping down an unhealthy tree if it needs to be removed.

PEST CONTROL

You're enjoying a peaceful evening with your family when you hear a scratching in the walls or you see something run across the floor. Unwanted pests like insects or rodents are attracted to your home for a variety of reasons including warmth in the fall and winter, or food crumbs you might have missed when sweeping up.

No one wants to live with pests in their home. A pest control expert can identify which pests are present, assess the extent of the problem and give you some strategies for resolution.

LOCKSMITHING

When your lock yourself out of your house or car, you call a locksmith to help you get back inside, but locksmiths do much more than that. These experts can also help you assess your security needs and help you find solutions appropriate for your home and lifestyle.

Perhaps you want something more than a standard doorknob lock. A locksmith can advise you on different types of locking mechanisms and home security strategies to give you peace of mind in knowing that your family will be safe. An expert locksmith will help you figure out the best plan, and is able to discuss other lock solutions such as a gun safe or a small vault for your valuables.

JUNK REMOVAL

Over time, it's easy to accumulate junk you don't need. After a thorough spring cleaning or renovation, you may have junk around your home that needs to be carted away, including old appliances, building materials, furniture and stuff the kids didn't take with them when they went off to college. Maybe it's too much or too big to simply drag to the curb. So what do you do with it?

Getting rid of major junk yourself requires a truck, physical labor and time. You also have to figure out whether you can take it all to the dump, or if it has to go to a recycling center or other location.

Employing the services of a junk removal expert is a fast, simple solution. You won't get dirty or strain your back, and you won't have to worry about whether there's a dump fee or if it will all fit. Plus, just think of all the free space you'll have in your house and garage when the job is done!

CLEANING SERVICES

How much time do you spend cleaning your house each week, time you could use doing other things you enjoy — going to the park, walking the dog, hanging out in the backyard or visiting friends and family.

When you consider how precious your time is, there's a lot of value in having someone else take care of cleaning your home. Thorough cleaning also improves your home's safety, comfort and value.

Whether you want regular help each week or just a deep cleaning every once in a while, our expert services offer convenience and peace of mind.

DECKS AND PATIOS

The sun is shining, it's a beautiful day and even though it's hot outside, your gorgeous deck or patio offers welcome shade where you and your family can sit and watch the kids play while sipping a cool beverage and listening to the birds. A deck or patio is an valuable asset to have in your home, a quiet, relaxing place to enjoy with your family and visitors, barbecue or read a book.

A deck and patio expert can look at your yard and advise on best choices and recommendations. Many of our clients are adding a small deck to the front of their homes, and a larger deck or a patio in the back to fit their lifestyles.

If you already have a deck, an expert can show you how to maintain and improve it to keep the space comfortable all year long.

LAWN IRRIGATION

Every lawn is different. For most people, watering it is something they do as an afterthought on a weekend if they remember. You know your lawn needs to be watered, but do you know how much or how often? It depends on the type of grass you have, the make-up of your soil and whether your lawn is shaded or in direct sun.

A lawn irrigation expert can install an irrigation system to ensure that your yard gets the water it needs when it needs it.

Just think — you never have to worry about watering your lawn again, and you never have to be embarrassed about having the driest, brownest lawn in the neighborhood. A lawn irrigation expert will help you find the right solution to achieve the greenest lawn on your street.

CARPET CLEANING

Carpets can be a functional way to add beauty and comfort to any room. However, they also act as giant filters that suck in all the dirt, dust, debris, dander, hair, germs and other particles that land on the floor. Over time, your carpet can start to look and smell unpleasant.

A professional cleaning can make a huge difference, drawing out dirt and grime to return your carpets to near new condition. Not only will your carpets be clean and look amazing, you won't be stirring up debris again every time you walk across them. Rely on the services of an expert to prolong the life of your carpeting.

DRIVEWAY REPAIR AND SEALING

Your driveway is a large flat surface usually made of concrete or asphalt. It looks beautiful when it's first installed, but over time it can start to deteriorate. Between the weight of your car and the movement of the ground due to extreme temperatures, your driveway can form cracks and dips and even degrade to the point where large chunks come out. When this happens, grass begins to grow and the cracks collect rainwater or snow, leading to further degradation.

To avoid this problem, you should have an expert regularly inspect your driveway and recommend appropriate treatment. You may want to have it sealed as a proactive measure against further cracks, or may do a large repair first and then seal as needed later.

You'll be amazed at how great your driveway looks when it's been repaired and sealed, and how an attractive driveway can really make the exterior of your house pop.

CHIMNEY CLEANING AND REPAIR

You probably don't think very much about your chimney, but it's important to consider for the safety and comfort of your family. A chimney from a woodstove, fireplace or a furnace is meant to draw smoke and carbon monoxide out of and away from your home. Over time, debris builds up on the inside of your chimney, making it harder for the chimney to operate effectively.

A chimney that is ignored for too long can become blocked completely, forcing smoke and carbon monoxide into your home and endangering your family. An expert can inspect your chimney and advise you on the best strategy for cleaning and repairs to keep it in safe working order.

DUCT SEALING WITH AEROSEAL

Heating and cooling can be expensive even if your home is relatively efficient, but if your air ducts aren't sealed properly, you could be wasting up to 40 percent of your homes energy. This increases utility bills and adds wear and tear to your HVAC system.

In addition to saving you energy and money, sealing your air ducts can prevent dust, pollen and other potential allergens from entering your system and degrading the indoor air quality. Aeroseal is a patented breakthrough technology that remedies duct leaks from the inside out. Homeowners are often amazed at the diagnostic measurement of their homes' leakage, and the improved comfort and money savings Aeroseal can provide.

RADON TESTING AND MITIGATION

According to estimates from the U.S. Environmental Protection Agency, radon causes as many as 21,000 lung cancer deaths annually, second only to smoking.
(https://www.epa.gov/sites/production/files/2016-12/documents/2016_a_citizens_guide_to_radon.pdf)

Caused by the breakdown of uranium in the soil, radon is a colorless, odorless gas that can seep into homes and buildings though gaps in the foundation. When radon leaks into a basement, it can pool there and permeate through the rest of the house, where it gets unknowingly ingested and inhaled by the occupants. Exposure to high concentrations of radon over time can result in serious health problems up to and including death.

Like oil and water, we know radon exists underneath the earth's surface, but there's no way to tell exactly where, how deep and how big the pockets are. In northern Colorado, ground disturbances due to fracking and construction can stir it up, and newer homes with well-sealed basements may actually be at greater risk than older homes with cracks that allow some of the gas to escape.

Knowing your radon measurement is the first step in keeping your family safe. Experts can measure the radon in your home and make recommendations on how to mitigate if the levels are too high.

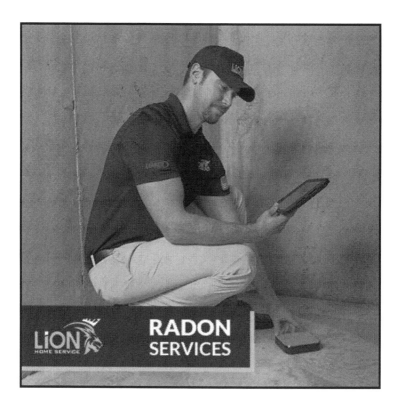

SEASONAL CHECKLISTS TO MAKE YOUR HOME SAFER AND MORE COMFORTABLE

Spring, summer, fall and winter — the seasons change like clockwork. We look forward to various aspects of each season, such as special events, holidays, vacations and the start of each new school year.

The seasons bring new opportunities, adventures and changes for your family, and they also effect changes to your house. If you want to make sure your home stays as safe and comfortable as it can all year long, there are a few simple maintenance tasks you should perform each season. These tasks are easy to do and many can be completed in an evening or over a weekend, especially if the whole family pitches in to help.

SPRING

Focus on freshening up your home and protecting your property against the season's strong winds and rains.

Outdoor tasks

- ☐ Clean gutters and downspouts. Learn how to maintain your gutters.
- ☐ Inspect roof and chimney for cracks and damage.
- ☐ Touch up peeling or damaged paint.
- ☐ Wash all windows, inside and out.
- ☐ Install screens on windows and doors.
- ☐ Clean outdoor furniture and air out cushions.
- ☐ Service your lawn mower.
- ☐ Fertilize your lawn.

Indoor tasks

- ☐ Test smoke and carbon monoxide detectors when you set clocks forward.
- ☐ Change the air filter on your furnace.
- ☐ If your basement has a sump pump, test it by dumping a large bucket of water into the basin of the sump pump. This should activate the sump pump. If it doesn't switch on, or if it's not pumping the water, it may need to be serviced by a

professional. Also, check for and remove any debris around the pump and make sure there are no leaks.

- ☐ Wash and change seasonal bedding.
- ☐ Dust blinds and vacuum curtains throughout your house.
- ☐ Clean out kitchen and bathroom cabinets. Throw away any outdated food, medicines and cosmetics.
- ☐ Inspect attic fan to make sure there are no animal nests, and test its performance.
- ☐ Have air conditioner professionally inspected.
- ☐ Test whole-home generator for proper function.
- ☐ Test panel circuit breakers.
- ☐ Test all home GFCI receptacles.
- ☐ Change water filters for water quality.

SUMMER

Complete the following projects to keep your yard lush and your home cool.

Outdoor tasks

- ☐ Walk around your home's exterior and slide open crawl space vents at the foundation.
- ☐ Prune trees and shrubs.
- ☐ Remove lint from dryer exhaust vent with a long, flexible brush.
- ☐ Uncover central air conditioner and install window air conditioners.

Indoor tasks

- ☐ Change or clean heating, ventilation and air conditioning filters. (Consult manufacturer instructions to determine whether you need to change filters more frequently.)
- ☐ Clean kitchen appliances inside and out, including refrigerator coils.
- ☐ Maintain clean drains by adding a half-cup of baking soda, followed by a half-cup of white vinegar. After 10 minutes, flush with boiling water.
- ☐ Drain or flush water heater.
- ☐ Test all GFCI receptacles.
- ☐ Change any water filters for water quality.

FALL

Prepare your home and yard for cooler temperatures, falling leaves and more time spent indoors.

Outdoor tasks

- ☐ Clean gutters and downspouts. Make sure drainage areas aren't blocked by leaves and debris. Consider installing gutter guards.
- ☐ Inspect your roof, or hire a licensed professional to examine your roof for wear and tear. If shingles are curling, buckling or cracking, it's time to replace them. In cases of extensive damage, replace the entire roof. Also, check the flashing around skylights, pipes and chimneys and make repairs as necessary. If you have leaks or gaps, heavy snow and ice will find its way in.
- ☐ Run your generator through a test cycle. Tune up if needed.
- ☐ Check basements and crawl spaces for signs of moisture and any cracks that need to be sealed.
- ☐ Close or install storm windows.
- ☐ Remove hoses from spigots. Drain, coil and store them flat in an indoor location.
- ☐ Store outdoor furniture and cushions.
- ☐ Test all outside floodlights and motion sensors.
- ☐ Use a screwdriver to probe wood trim around windows, doors, railings and decks. Use caulk to fill holes or completely replace the wood.
- ☐ To prevent exterior water pipes from bursting in below-freezing temperatures, turn off the valves to the exterior hose bibs. Run the water until the pipes are empty. Make sure all water is drained from the pipes.
- ☐ Lower humidity and cooler (but not yet cold) temperatures make fall a good time to paint the exterior of your home.

Indoor tasks

- ☐ Check grout and silicone in bathtubs and showers. Seal if needed.
- ☐ Have furnace professionally inspected.
- ☐ Test sump pump and the battery back-up for proper operation.

- ☐ Change the air filter on your furnace.
- ☐ Inspect ducts to see if duct cleaning is needed (Recommendation: Do this before major allergies hit!)
- ☐ Check indicator lights on all home surge protectors.
- ☐ Test all home GFCI receptacles.
- ☐ Change water filters for water quality.
- ☐ Test smoke alarms and carbon monoxide detectors.
- ☐ Vacuum lint from the clothes dryer.
- ☐ Vacuum condenser coils to increase energy efficiency.

WINTER

Enjoy energy-efficient warmth and the fruits of your home-maintenance labors. Thoroughly clean and care for your home's interior while taking a few precautionary measures on the outside.

Outdoor tasks

- ☐ Walk around your home's exterior and check the crawl space vents located at the foundation. Close any that are open.
- ☐ Protect your central air conditioning unit with a cover.
- ☐ Remove and store window air conditioners.
- ☐ Clean and store garden tools.
- ☐ Move snow shovels and snow blowers to a convenient spot for use. Stock up on ice melting compound for walkways.
- ☐ Inspect your roof for loose tiles and shingles and signs of leaks around vents, skylights and chimneys. Check around your foundation for signs of moisture and cracks.
- ☐ Touch up any paint that's cracking or peeling.
- ☐ Clean out gutters and downspouts to remove leaves and other blockages.
- ☐ Clean out the chimney to remove buildup of flammable substances. Have a professional inspect your chimney every year to prevent fire hazards during the winter months.

Indoor tasks

- ☐ Change or clean furnace filters.
- ☐ Clean kitchen appliances inside and out, including refrigerator coils.
- ☐ Maintain clean drains with BioClean product.

- ☐ Drain the water heater until it's clear of sediment and refill with clean water.
- ☐ Clean grill and fan blades on exhaust fans.
- ☐ Flush your garbage disposal with hot water and baking soda.
- ☐ Lubricate hinges and moving parts on all doors and windows.
- ☐ Shampoo carpets and wax floors.

PART 4.

COMMON PROBLEMS AND WHAT TO DO ABOUT THEM

When your furnace stops working, you know it's time to call in an expert who can repair or replace it, but there are many times when issues occur around the house that you may not even realize could benefit from expert help! You just learn to live with the inconvenience or cost or risk. Or perhaps you just aren't aware that an expert can take care of it for you quickly.

In this part of the book, we'll look at a number of common problems that can occur around your house, and you'll discover that an expert may be able to help you with more than you realize.

At the very end of this section, I've provided a helpful checklist you can use to go through your home and identify areas that might need work.

COMMON PROBLEMS AND CONCERNS AROUND YOUR HOME

When any major home system stops working, you know it's time to call in an expert. There are often many other minor things that need work, but you just learn to live with them. Do any of these examples sound familiar?

- A power receptacle stops working.
- There are hot and cold spots in the house.
- Your laundry room is too dark.
- You never realized the danger of a power surge and the damage it could do to your electronics.

Those are just a few things we live with every day. We just don't use the power receptacle that stops working, or we just squint when we're doing laundry.

It doesn't have to be that way. Your home is your castle, and it should be the place where life is simple and convenient, not where you have to work around problems.

Read through this part of the book and see if any of these situations are happening in your home.

I always advise all members of the household to go through this section of the book at the same time, perhaps after dinner one evening. It won't take long. The reason I suggest this — you may not notice the same things your spouse or kids do.

One of my customers went to work every day while his wife stayed home to look after their two young children. He thought his home's temperature was fine, but his wife pointed out that the children's playroom was never quite as warm as the rest of the house. The customer didn't know this because he often played with his children outside in the evenings.

Another client didn't realize that one of the bathroom sinks had been clogged for months until his teenage children mentioned it.

Sit down with your family and go through this part of the book to see if any of these situations are happening in your home right now.

COMMON PROBLEMS WITH YOUR HOME'S TEMPERATURE

In this chapter, we'll look at common problems with your home's temperature, explore some of the possible causes and determine what you can do about it. In some cases, we'll provide ideas and tips to help you decide what to do; in other cases, you may need to contact a licensed expert for help.

Because homes vary so much from one area to the next, we are only able to provide general recommendations. If you're not sure what the problem is or what to do about it, have a licensed expert take a look at the situation for you. Even calling our office and talking to an expert over the phone may help you figure out the problem.

No matter what, your family's safety is the most important thing. Don't attempt anything dangerous if you are not sure what the outcome might be.

HVAC systems are built to high standards with many safeguards in place, and they're very safe when installed by a licensed professional. If you're worried about the safety of your family, leave the house immediately with your children and pets and contact a licensed HVAC expert for help.

These are some common problems that homeowners experience with regard to the temperature:

My house is too cold.

- Consider whether this condition is normal, or if it's a new development. If your house is always cold, it might mean that you need a new, bigger furnace or duct sealing. If it's a new development, there could be a temporary problem with your furnace.
- Check to make sure all doors and windows are closed tight.
- Check the weather-stripping around doors and windows.
- Check to make sure your furnace is running. Is it plugged in? Is the breaker on your circuit panel closed?
- Check the furnace filter to see if it's clean.
- Check to make sure there's nothing blocking the vents.
- Contact a licensed HVAC expert for help.

My furnace is making an unusual noise.

- Try to determine the source of the noise. Is it coming from the furnace itself? Is it coming from the ductwork elsewhere in the house?
- Try to narrow down when the noise occurs. Does the sound happen consistently? Does it happen only when the furnace is about to turn on to heat the house, or about to turn off once your house has reached the right temperature?
- Think about how you'd describe the noise. Is it a metallic rattling? A hissing? A buzzing?
- Contact a licensed HVAC expert for help.

I smell dust or smoke whenever my furnace comes on.

- Check your furnace air filter and clean or replace it if it's dirty.
- If the filter is clean and you still smell dust or smoke, there may be dust in your ducts that needs to be cleaned out.
- Contact a licensed HVAC expert for help.

My house is too hot.

- Consider whether this condition is normal, or if it's a new development. If your house is always hot, it might mean that you need a new, bigger air conditioner or duct sealing. If it's a new development, there could be a temporary problem with your air conditioner.
- Check your air conditioning system to see if it's plugged in and running. If it's plugged in but not running, check the circuit panel and reset the breaker.
- Check the filter to see if it's dirty and needs to be cleaned or replaced.
- Check the ducts and vents to ensure there are no blockages.
- Contact a licensed HVAC expert for help.

COMMON PROBLEMS WITH YOUR HOME'S ELECTRICAL SYSTEM

In this chapter, we'll look at common problems that you may face with your home's electrical system, explore some of the possible causes and determine what you can do about them. In some cases, we'll provide ideas and tips to help you decide what to do; in other cases, you may need to contact a licensed expert for help.

My receptacles or fan/lights aren't working.

- Check the light or the electronic device that's plugged into the receptacle. Make sure the light bulb hasn't blown, or there isn't something defective with the device itself. For example, try the bulb in another light in a different room, or try plugging your electronic device into a receptacle in a different room.
- Check to see if a circuit needs to be reset, and reset if necessary.
- If neither of these things work, contact a licensed expert.

COMMON PROBLEMS WITH YOUR HOME'S PLUMBING SYSTEM

In this chapter, we'll look at common problems that you may face with your home's plumbing, explore some of the possible causes and determine what you can do about them. In some cases, we'll provide ideas and tips to help you decide what to do; in other cases, you may need to contact a licensed expert for help.

My faucets are leaking.
- Make sure taps are fully turned off.
- If your faucet continues to leak, contact a licensed expert.

There's water dripping from a pipe.
- Place a bucket under the drip.
- See if you can locate the source. It may not always be directly under the drip. A leak may occur at a higher part of the pipe, but the water will drip off the lowest area of the pipe.
- Turn off the nearest valve if there is one, or turn off your home's main water intake valve.

My hot water isn't very hot.
- Determine whether another hot water source has recently drained your hot water tank. For example, are you trying to take a shower shortly after doing a large load of laundry?
- Determine whether you water needs have recently changed. For example, your family of four usually has an adequate hot water supply, but when you have guests, not everyone gets a hot shower.
- Check to see if your hot water tank's temperature setting is still at the recommended position.
- Check to see if your hot water tank is operating (for instance, if it's a gas-powered tank, is the pilot light on?) Restart the system if possible.
- Think about when you last flushed your hot water tank.
- If the setting is where it's always been and if the tank seems to be operating normally, contact an expert for help.

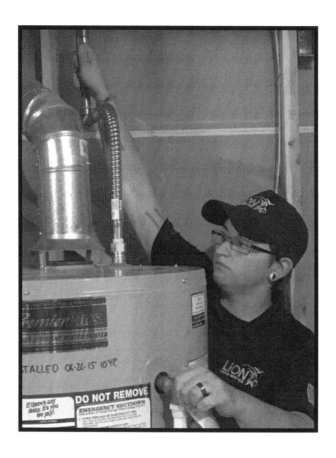

COMMON PROBLEMS WITH YOUR HOME'S DRAIN/SEWER/SEPTIC SYSTEM

In this chapter, we'll look at common problems that you may face with your home's drain/sewer/septic system, explore some of the possible causes and determine what you can do about them. In some cases, we'll provide ideas and tips to help you decide what to do; in other cases, you may need to contact a licensed expert for help.

My toilet isn't draining.
- Plunge your toilet, then carefully dump a bucket of water into the bowl.
- If that doesn't work to clear the drain, contact an expert for help.

My sink or bathtub drain isn't draining.
- Check to make sure there's nothing blocking the drain such as a plug, debris, hair, a toy, etc.
- If possible, pour baking soda down the drain followed by white vinegar. You should only do this if the sink or tub is not too full. If you can get to the drain easily, try this.
- If these measures don't work, contact an expert for help.

CHECKLIST OF COMMON PROBLEMS AROUND YOUR HOME

Homes need regular check-up, just like we do, to ensure proper efficiency. Use this checklist to identify features of your home that could be made safer and more comfortable for your family.

- ☐ Are you concerned about utility bills going up as your furnace, boiler, water heater or air conditioner age?
- ☐ Does your family suffer from allergies or other breathing troubles?
- ☐ Are you frustrated by temperature differences (e.g., some areas of your home are hot while other areas are cold)?

☐ Have the ducts in your home been cleaned recently to remove dust and allergens?

☐ Can you control your thermostat when you're away; or do you get worried about unnecessary heating bills or frozen pipes?

☐ Has your heating and/or cooling equipment become annoyingly loud and noisy during start-up or shutdown?

☐ Do you get frustrated because the house is never the right temperature during the winter or summer?

☐ Does your attic get very hot and humid during the summer months?

☐ Have you detected mold in your attic?

☐ Are you concerned about switches or plugs that are warm to the touch? Are there any outlets that feel loose when you're plugging in or unplugging something?

☐ Are you aggravated by a breaker that keeps tripping?

☐ Have you ever had to endure the expense and hassle of replacing appliances or electronics due to a power surge?

☐ Are there areas in your home where you have to run extension cords and could use another outlet?

☐ Do you have any annoyingly slow-draining sinks, tubs or toilets? (Note: even if they're working right now, has this occurred within the last five years?)

☐ Does your home suffer from hard water, causing white build up on your plumbing? Are you worried about the impact this could have on your family's health?

☐ Are you concerned about what your children are drinking when they fill a glass from the tap or brush their teeth?

☐ Do you run out of hot water for showers and baths more quickly than you would like?

☐ Are you worried that your basement will be ruined from a sump pump failure due to a power outage?

☐ Are you concerned about your family's health because of damp walls, mold and musty odors in the basement?

☐ Do you experience flickering lights, unexpected dimming or frequently burned out bulbs?

If you've checked any items off this list, contact Lion Home Service today to solve the problem for you right away.

PART 5.

HOW TO FIND A TRUSTED EXPERT TO HELP YOU SAVE MONEY, SAVE TIME, ELIMINATE STRESS, AND MAKE YOUR HOME SAFER AND MORE COMFORTABLE FOR YOUR FAMILY

You've determined that your home needs to be serviced by a professional, but how do you know who to hire? There are many home service companies out there, how do you know which one to choose? Or should you just ask your cousin to fix the problem because he's handy around the house?

In this chapter of the book, you'll learn how to make better decisions for your home and find out who's best qualified to make your home safer and more comfortable for your family.

HOW TO MAKE WISE DECISIONS FOR YOUR HOME

Life is busy. You go to work, you go to the grocery store, you take the kids to soccer practice. If your family is like many others, you barely have time to catch your breath!

For this reason, some things get put on the back burner. Maybe you don't pursue hobbies as much as you used to, or you don't get to spend as much time outdoors as you'd like. Maybe you don't get to visit friends as often as you did before you had kids or grandkids.

Sometimes, home maintenance takes a back burner, too. You're so busy making decisions, paying bills, getting dinner on the table and making sure the dog's been fed that you don't have five spare minutes to think about your home.

You're not alone. The good thing is, most of your home's systems tend to run themselves for the most part. You don't have to worry about them too much and can simply get on with your life. But sometimes, a problem occurs and you DO have to think about your home. Maybe your HVAC system isn't producing as much heat as it used to, or a drain suddenly backs up.

Now what? All of a sudden, your home become a top priority. You need your house to be safe and comfortable for your family and if a problem occurs, it's easy to feel frustrated, stressed and overwhelmed. You're already busy with the other aspects of life, and now you need to find a quick solution to another problem!

When a problem occurs in your home, you can turn to this chapter to help you make the best decisions for your home and family. We've included a simple step-by-step way to evaluate the problem and to reach a solution quickly without a lot of stress.

Think of this as a simple checklist to run through whenever you encounter a challenge with your home. Answer each question in the list below, and by the time you're done, you'll have a game plan to get the problem solved and get your life back on track.

First, identify the situation. For example, maybe the house isn't as warm or cool as it needs to be. Maybe the faucet is dripping. Maybe you're not experiencing a critical problem, but you just want to upgrade your bathroom.

Second, identify the source of the problem. This isn't always possible, but if you can, try to trace the problem to its source. Your leaky faucet is probably exactly what you think it is, but a clogged drain could be caused by a problem further down the pipe. In this case, you'll need to find out if just one drain isn't working, or if all the drains in your home are clogged.

Third, determine if what's happening presents a safety issue now, or could lead to one. Your family's safety is important. If the problem that's occurring is a safety issue right now, or if you think it could lead to one, you'll want to deal with it right away. Remember, just because it may not be a safety issue today doesn't mean it won't turn into one down the road.

Fourth, determine if what's happening is a comfort issue now, or could lead to one in the future. You want your home to be comfortable. If something is disrupting the comfort of your family, you'll want to get it fixed quickly. Some comfort issues could also become health and safety issues down the road. For example, if your HVAC system stops working and your house doesn't warm up, it's a comfort issue. If it continues and your pipes freeze and burst, now you've got an incredibly costly problem on your hands that could lead to a damp, moldy basement.

Fifth, determine whether your home's value will be impacted by the problem. While safety and comfort are often higher priorities, your home is a significant investment and you'll want to make decisions based on the impact they can potentially have on its value. For example, your HVAC system might work just fine, but upgrading to a more modern high-efficiency model help preserve or increase the overall value of your home.

Sixth, understand the value of hiring an expert. Many homeowners want to find the right service provider. Some simply end up choosing the company with the cheapest estimate, but not necessarily the company who'll do the best job. There are many different service providers out there, and not all of them are the same. In the upcoming chapters of this book, we'll share some tips on how to compare and measure the differences between one service provider and another.

Seventh, understand the impact of taking action today. When life gets busy, it's easy to gloss over the things that don't seem to be big issues right now. However, delaying action can actually cost you more than fixing the problem quickly. For example, repairing a leaky faucet today is less expensive than waiting until the problem gets bigger:

- The cost of water leaking out of your faucets will continue until the faucet is repaired.
- The cost of parts rise.
- The repair company might be experiencing a busy season. By the time you decide to take action, they may not be able to come out as soon as you need them.

Taking action today is always cheaper than waiting.

Here's The Bottom Line

If you want to make wise decisions for your family, consider the questions above and use them to help you formulate a game plan.

You don't have to spend a long time on these questions, but answering them will help you get the processing moving toward solving the situation and making your home safer and more comfortable for your family.

ARE YOU MEASURING THE WRONG THING?

Coworkers and friends, Alan and Barb both happen to be shopping for a car at the same time. They're both conscientious consumers who want to make the smartest purchase for their families.

After careful shopping, Alan finds three cars he likes. They all seem similar, so he selects the cheapest option. At the same time, Barb finds three cars that she likes. They all seem similar, too, but after doing some additional research, Barb goes with the most expensive option.

Alan laughs at Barb and tells her that she got ripped off. After all, he only paid a fraction of the price for his car that Barb paid for hers. Then Alan's tire goes flat. Turns out, the tires on the car he purchased were worn out, but cheaper than the new tires on Barb's car.

Then Alan's car overheats. It turns out there was a leak in the radiator, and the repair isn't covered because Alan chose not to spend extra money on a warranty. Then the battery dies and needs to be replaced. Then a sensor goes out. Alan needs to replace a headlight, and his brakes start to squeal.

Alan takes his car back to the dealership and complains, accusing them of selling him a lemon. But the dealership doesn't take returns. Alan is simply stuck.

Meanwhile, Barb has no trouble at all with her car, and picks Alan up to take him to work when his car breaks down.

One year later, they both add up what they've spent on their respective cars. Barb may have spent more upfront to buy her car, but Alan — who pinched pennies and thought he was getting the better deal — actually spent more in the long run.

This situation happens every single day in many different scenarios:

- People buy discount clothes that wear out faster than a quality product, and have to spend more to replace them sooner.

- People buy budget services that simply don't fulfill what they need, and then have to either make do or spend more to get more services.
- People buy the gadget with the lowest price and it stops working sooner, so they spend more to replace it over and over again. Or, they shell out more for repairs.

Many people haven't learned the difference between value and price. Value is the **benefit** you get from something; price is the **amount** you pay for something. Both of these are important factors to consider when making any purchase. However, some people focus solely on price and ignore the value they're getting. As a result, they wind up paying more in the long run to make up for it.

Here's a rule of thumb you should always keep in mind when making a purchase: **Buy for the value. When faced with a choice between offerings of equal value, choose the lowest price.**

That's what Barb did in the story above. She bought for the value the car provided. Her additional research revealed that the cars were not of equal value, so she purchased the car that provided the best value. Alan did the opposite and bought a car without considering the value; he just bought the car at the lower price.

Here's why this matters to homeowners. Your home is an investment, and if you want to protect it and even potentially increase its value, you need to invest in your home's maintenance. If you're only basing decisions on price, you run the risk of buying something that could actually cost you more in the long run. Buying based on value will save you money and frustration.

As home service professionals, we often meet people who want to get at least three price quotes before making a decision. There's nothing wrong with being informed or getting quotes to compare. But, we also get calls from people who tell us, "I chose to hire someone else because their quote was lower than yours, but they did a terrible job. Can you come back and fix their mistake?"

If you're comparing estimates and deciding who to hire to work on your home, the most important thing to consider is the value you'll be getting for your money. Don't just look at the price. Consider what the company promises you — that's the value. Then hire the best experts based on the value they bring.

Of course, if you have estimates of equal value, it makes sense to choose the lowest price. But you'll rarely find estimates of equal value because all home service companies are not the same.

REAL INTEGRITY IS DOING THE RIGHT THING, KNOWING THAT NOBODY'S GOING TO KNOW WHETHER YOU DID IT OR NOT.

WHO CAN HELP YOU THE BEST?

Life can get very busy. Between work, soccer practice for the kids, social life, volunteer commitments, grocery shopping and date night with your partner, there's really not much time for anything else. That's why you love your home, because it offers a comfortable oasis away from the busy outside world.

When something breaks or you're trying to be proactive with maintenance, it can be hard to know what to do and who to trust to help you. Should you try to fix something yourself? Should you call your friend who knows a thing or two about plumbing? Should you open the Yellow Pages and just call the first company you see? Should you call the cheapest company? Should you call an expert?

Asking these questions ahead of time before a disaster strikes is a great way to prepare yourself for any situation.

In this chapter, we'll explore each of these questions.

Should you try to fix something yourself?

When a problem arises with the systems in your home, there are a few things you can do to correct the problem, or at least to narrow down the problem before you call for help.

For example, checking to make sure your ducts aren't blocked, resetting the breaker in your circuit panel, plunging the toilet or going over to the neighbor's house to see if they're experiencing the same water discoloration you are — these are all quick, simple and safe things you can do right away that may solve the problem or help you inform a licensed expert when you schedule an appointment.

Never, ever risk doing anything that's unsafe! If you're not sure, don't do it. Instead, call a licensed expert who can walk you through some simple options or send help to you.

Should you call your friend who knows a thing or two?

After working for more than two decades in the home services industry, I can tell you that this happens all the time. For example, Joe doesn't know a lot about plumbing, but his friend Bob does. So Joe calls Bob and asks him for help installing a new pipe and faucet for a dishwasher. Bob comes over to help and the two of them get to work. Seems pretty simple, right?

Bob leaves and goes home. A week or two passes, then Joe wakes up in the middle of the night to a strange noise. The pipe that Bob installed has ruptured and is spewing water all of Joe's expensively renovated basement.

What recourse options does Joe have? He could try to sue Bob, but that's time consuming and costly. There's no contract in place, and who knows if Bob has the money to cover the bill?

Should you open the Yellow Pages or do an online search and just call the first company you see?

Many people do this, but it's not a good idea. The Yellow Pages are arranged in alphabetical order, which means you may overlook a great company whose name starts with the letter Z because you called a mediocre company that starts with the letter A.

And, if you choose to call only the companies with big, colorful ads, you're not necessarily calling the best company; you're simply calling the company that's willing to spend the most money on advertising.

Consider this. Would you rather go to a doctor because he'll make you healthy, or because his last name starts with the letter A and he's got the money to buy a big ad?

Should you call the cheapest company?

A penny saved is a penny earned, right? You work hard for your money, and you should carefully manage what you spend it on.

Many homeowners believe that all home service companies are the same — a plumber is a plumber, at least in the eyes of the layperson. So if you get three estimates and one is significantly lower than the others, doesn't it make sense to go with the lowest price?

I caution you to be careful when comparing estimates and simply choosing the company with the lowest quote. ALL ELSE BEING EQUAL, it makes sense to choose the lowest-priced option. If there are two cars that are EXACTLY the same on a dealership lot and one costs $100 less than the other, it makes perfect sense to choose the cheaper one.

However, the key message here is "All else being equal." Something you should know and may not be aware of — most home services companies are NOT equal. Sure, two plumbers or two electricians working for two different home service companies might have the same qualifications, and those two companies might even look similar at first glance. But, there are many differences between home service companies, and price should only be one of the deciding factors.

You should also consider factors like:

- How long the company has been in business
- What the company's customer service rating is
- Whether the company is A+ rated with the Better Business Bureau

- What kind of service the company delivers before, during, and after the work is done
- What kind of values the company follows
- Whether the company offers expertise in the specific services you need
- … and more. (See the decision-making checklist in the next chapter.)

You should always choose the BEST company for your home, not necessarily the one that offers you the lowest price. Remember, employing a home service company is an investment in the safety and comfort of your family, and in the value (and resale value) of your home.

Consider these two examples of what can happen when you go with the cheapest option:

- Donna got three estimates and chose the cheapest one. The tech showed up, but instead of getting to work, upsold her on a much larger unit than what was quoted in his original estimate. This "bait-and-switch" tactic allowed the tech to win the project with a lower bid, but ultimately charge a higher price.
- Jack got three estimates and chose the one with the cheapest hourly rate. Unfortunately, what Jack didn't realize is that the company with the cheapest hourly rate didn't hire the best employees. What would have taken any other company one or two hours to repair took the cheaper company three to five hours to repair, ultimately running up the repair bill higher (and taking up more time) than if Jack had hired one of the higher-priced companies from the start.

Should you call an expert?

Hiring an expert is the best solution for these reasons:

- An expert gives you the confidence that the problem will be solved. Period.

- An expert gives you confidence that the problem will be solved safely.
- An expert will get the job faster, ultimately saving you money.
- An expert will proactively advise you on other potential problems or opportunities to make your home safer and more comfortable.
- An expert will never be pushy or use tricky sales tactics, but will advise you of your options and allow you to make the best decision for your family without pressure.
- An expert will be fully trained.
- An expert will be licensed.
- An expert will be drug-tested and background-checked.
- An expert will be insured.
- An expert will be professional. You don't have to send the kids out of the house because of something an expert might say!
- An expert will have clear identification so you know you can safely let them into your house.
- An expert will have all the proper documentation and help guide you through any permitting requirements.

DECISION-MAKING CHECKLIST

When faced with a decision about your home's safety and comfort systems (including HVAC, electrical, plumbing, drain/sewer, waterproofing, home security and automation, bathroom solutions, water purification, indoor air quality, generators and more), you have a lot of choices to consider.

In the last chapter, you read about the reasons to call a professional company with experts who can help you. But when you open the Yellow Pages or go online, it seems like there are a lot of professional companies out there!

In this chapter, you'll get a simple, clear decision-making checklist that can help you find the very best professional home service expert for your needs.

The checklist is simple and works like this:

1. Select three to five local companies you think might be able to help you.
2. Answer these questions for each company.
3. Choose the company that earns the best score.

In just a few minutes you'll have the best answer to your question, "*Which professional home services company can best help me make my home safer and more comfortable?*"

You can also download a larger version of this checklist at HomeownersNewswire.com/homeownerschecklist

The decision-making checklist to help you find an expert to make your home safer and more comfortable

	Compare our company and two other companies by ranking them based on the factors below.	Company A	Company B	Company C
1.	Are they a branded and recognizable company? (Or have you never heard of them before?)	Y/N	Y/N	Y/N
2.	How long have they been in business?	—	—	—
3.	Who owns the company? (An original owner or a franchiser?)	—	—	—
4.	How many customers have they served?	—	—	—
5.	Are they licensed, bonded and insured?	Y/N	Y/N	Y/N
6.	Are they recognized with an A+ rating by the Better Business Bureau?	Y/N	Y/N	Y/N
7.	Are they part of a recognizable group that helps and supports homeowners (such as HomeownersNewswire.com)?	Y/N	Y/N	Y/N
8.	What are their hours of operation?	—	—	—
9.	Are team members cross-trained in different home systems?	Y/N	Y/N	Y/N
10.	Are team members experts in what they	Y/N	Y/N	Y/N

	do?			
11.	Are all team members drug-tested and background searched?	Y/N	Y/N	Y/N
12.	Do team members have company identification?	Y/N	Y/N	Y/N
13.	Do team members use floormats and boot protectors on the job?	Y/N	Y/N	Y/N
14.	Does the company have testimonials to offer from other satisfied homeowners (whether on their web site or on social media)?	Y/N	Y/N	Y/N
	Which company has the best results? *(See scoring instructions below)*	—	—	—

Scoring instructions:

For Y/N questions: Y = 3 points; N = 0 points

For all other questions: award 3 points to the best answer, 2 points to the middle answer, and 1 point to the worst answer. (Or zero points if you don't know the answer).

For example: Company A served 140,000 customers, Company B served 60,000 customers, and Company C didn't reveal how many customers they served.

4.	How many customers have they served?	140K	60K	???

You would give 3 points to Company A, 2 points to Company B, and 0 points to Company C.

Now simply add up the points for each company and place that number at the bottom of the chart, like this:

Which company has the best results? *(See scoring instructions below)*	43	28	10

The higher number, the better! Now you have a simple, at-a-glance way to see which company is best qualified to help you make your home safer and more comfortable for your family.

HERE'S THE SURPRISING THING NO ONE TELLS YOU (AND IT CAN SAVE YOU A LOT OF HASSLE!)

When our experts show up at customers' homes because something has broken down, one of the things we often hear is, "I didn't realize this wasn't working properly until it broke."

You lead a busy life and chances are, you probably don't spend a lot of time thinking about your HVAC, plumbing or electrical system, until it stops working. There's nothing wrong with not paying a lot of attention to these systems. You have a lot to think about and, for the most part, these systems usually work just fine on their own.

When they stop working the way you want them to, that's when the hassle starts. You go to the Internet and search for what's wrong, or you call up a friend to ask for an opinion or a quick assessment. The problem is, investigating is hard to do when you're not an expert and you're just trying to find out what the problem is. It's even worse in the case of an emergency, such as water rushing into your basement. You don't know why it's happening or where it's coming from, and the Internet or that friend won't be able to help you very much.

Let's say you have an extremely sore elbow, but instead of going to the doctor, you search online for information. There are many reasons why your elbow could be sore, and you really need an expert to assess the situation.

Fortunately, there's a simple solution to solve this problem, and by using this simple solution:

- You've save money by avoiding mistakes and wrong decisions.
- You'll save even more money by proactively addressing problems before they become large and costly.
- You'll save time because you can make faster decisions (and they won't be rushed).
- You'll eliminate hassle and doubt by thinking through a solution with all the information.
- You'll make your home safer and more comfortable, and keep it that way.

The secret is: Find a trusted expert who can help with all of your home's systems and services, and then build a relationship with that expert to proactively care for your home.

Maybe that sounds weird because in the past, you've only ever called a home service company when you needed to address something immediate — a burst pipe, an HVAC repair or a water heater upgrade.

But here's the secret that some people know, and it saves them time, money and stress — your home service expert is a lot like your mechanic or your family doctor. Some people only go to a mechanic or doctor when something's wrong. Smart people go for regular check-ups even when they're not experiencing any negative symptoms. Here's why:

- When the expert sees things are running normally and becomes familiar with your home and its systems, it provides a baseline of knowledge, just like a mechanic might need to know about how your car performs under the best conditions to provide the most appropriate service, or like what your doctor needs to know about how your body functions when you're well and healthy.
- The expert has tools and strategies that can detect potential issues before they become bigger, catastrophic, costlier problems.
- The expert can make proactive suggestions about ways to increase the safety and comfort of your home based on what they know about your family.

This is only possible when you build a relationship with a home services expert. The expert comes to your house and sees things working normally. You can sit down and discuss what your home is like and what your goals are to provide safety and comfort for your family. (Conversely, this doesn't happen if you only ever call the first available home service company to come over right away because your water heater just burst all over your basement.)

Schedule an expert come in and do regular check-ups on your home. This proactive approach goes a long way toward enhancing the safety and comfort of your home.

We can't recommend this strongly enough. If you only take one single action after reading this book: **Find a trusted home services company and have an expert visit your home to do a home services check-up every six months.**

Imagine the peace of mind you'll feel when you see this truck pull up in your driveway…

Our team is ready to serve you. We want to make your home safe and comfortable for your family, and we'll do everything we can to "wow" you with our service.

Do you have a friend, relative, neighbor or coworker we can "wow" as well? Next time you hear someone complaining about a leaky faucet or worrying about the quality of water their family is drinking, tell them to call us.

ABOUT THE AUTHOR

Barton Palmer was raised in Montrose, Colorado and earned a degree in finance from Colorado State University. In 1998, he launched his career in home construction services, later becoming a Ben Franklin franchisee.

In May 2018, Bart founded Lion Home Service in Fort Collins to provide complete home solutions, from electrical, heating and cooling to water treatment, insulation, and other services. The company is one of the largest home services providers in Northern Colorado.

Under Bart's direction, Lion Home Service supports Realities for Children, funding the unmet needs of abused, neglected and at-risk youth in Larimer County through 34 partner agencies.

Bart regularly contributes content to the Coloradoan newspaper and to Homeowners Newswire, the No. 1 resource for homeowners who want a safer and more comfortable home for their families.

An avid home cook, Bart enjoys spending time with his son, Joseph and Jacob.

GET IN TOUCH WITH US

1-833-403-LION (5466)

LionHomeService.com

info@LionHomeService.com

Our call center is open 24/7 and is staffed by local experts who can help you right away. We offer evening and weekend service at no extra charge.

Visit and bookmark our web site for more tips and ideas to help you enjoy a safer, more comfortable home for your family.

While you're there, enter your email address for immediate access to money-saving coupons for many of the services you need around your home.

LionHomeService.com